Sexual Force
or
the Winged Dragon

Translated from the French
Original title: LA FORCE SEXUELLE
OU LE DRAGON AILÉ

Omraam Mikhaël Aïvanhov

Sexual Force
or
the Winged Dragon

5th edition
Second printing March 2000

Izvor Collection — No. 205

P R O S V E T A

Canadian Cataloguing in Publication Data

Aïvanhov, Omraam Mikhaël, 1900-1986
    Sexual force or the winged dragon

        (Izvor collection ; 205)
        Translation of: La force sexuelle ou le dragon ailé.
        ISBN 1-895978-12-2

        1. Love. 2. Sex--Philosophy. I. Title. II. Series: Izvor
    collection (North Hatley, Quebec) ; 205.

BD436.A3913 2000   128'.46   C00-900441-6

Prosveta Inc.
3950, Albert Mines, North Hatley, QC, Canada J0B 2C0

        Prosveta S.A. — B.P. 12 — 83601 Fréjus Cedex (France)

TABLE OF CONTENTS

1

THE WINGED DRAGON

We find the figure of the snake or dragon in all folk stories of popular traditions, in fairy tales and mythology, and its symbolism is similar in all cultures. Countless fairy tales tell of a dragon which captures a beautiful princess and then keeps his pure and innocent prisoner captive in a castle. The poor princess, languishing in her gaol, weeps as she begs Heaven to send someone to save her. Knights gallop up to rescue her, but one after another they are devoured by the dragon, who seizes all their wealth and then hoards it in the castle cellars. However, one fine day, a knight rides up; he is a prince, more noble, handsome and pure than all the others. A witch has told him the secret by which he can conquer the dragon : she has revealed the dragon's weakness and told him how and when he will be able to bind or wound the dragon.... So the lucky prince, well provided with weapons and information, wins the victory. He frees the princess, and then what gentle kisses they give each other! All the treasures stored in the castle for centuries are now given to the handsome prince who has triumphed because of his knowledge and his purity. Prince and princess climb onto the dragon's back and fly all over the universe.

People often think that these fairy stories are for children only. In fact, they are Initiatic tales; in order to understand them, you need to know the science of symbols. The dragon is the sexual force. The castle is the human body. The unhappy princess who has been held prisoner by uncontrolled sexual energy is the soul. The knight is the ego or the spirit of man. The arms he uses to conquer the dragon are the weapons of the spirit – willpower and knowledge, used to control this energy. So then, once the dragon has been mastered, it becomes man's servant, his mount for journeys through space, because this dragon has wings. Pictures always give the dragon a serpent's tail, the symbol of subterranean forces, but he also has wings. The eternal language of symbols is so clear and simple!

There is a variant of this story to be found in the myth of Theseus. Ariadne gave Theseus a golden thread and, thanks to this, he was able to guide himself through the labyrinth, kill the Minotaur, and then find his way out of the labyrinth once more. The Minotaur is another representation of the sexual force, of the lower nature, which, like the powerful and prolific bull, has to be yoked and harnessed to till the soil. The labyrinth (the castle) represents the physical body and Ariadne represents the Higher Self which shows man the way to victory.

In Jewish and Christian traditions, the dragon is likened to the Devil and the Devil, they say, smells of sulphur. All inflammable products such as petrol, oil, gunpowder, mixtures of gas which produce flames and explosions, all these are the fire-breathing Dragon in Nature. The Dragon also exists in man ; once again he can be seen in all man's combustible qualities. If, through ignorance, carelessness or weakness, man does not know how to make use of these combustible forces, he will find that, instead of being propelled towards Heaven, he will be hurled into the abyss or reduced to ashes.

2

LOVE AND SEXUALITY

I

"Master, will you tell us what difference you see between love and sexuality and show us how sexuality can be used in the spiritual life?"

You are asking a very interesting question which touches on the most important thing in life and affects everybody, both young and old.

I would not say that I am qualified to answer all the questions that arise from this problem. However, I do have something slightly special which is that I always like to see things from a particular point of view and I have dedicated all my life to acquiring this point of view. I would just like to say a few words to you about this so that you do not start criticizing me and saying, "Oh my goodness, I have read books on love and sexuality which say much more. What an ignorant teacher!" I am not afraid of admitting my ignorance. However, those who write the books you mention do not have my point of view and do not understand the question as I do. You can, if you so wish, get all the information available on sexuality as written by psychoanalysts and doctors, but I wish to lead you towards another point of view which has been unknown up to now.

What is this point of view? I give you the following image to explain what I mean. Picture a professor, a graduate of three or four universities. He is working in his laboratory doing all sorts of research experiments.... His twelve year old son out in the garden climbs a tree and from the top calls out, "Daddy, I can see my uncle and aunt coming along the road!" His father, who can see nothing, asks, "How far away are they? What are they carrying?" and the child gives him all the information. Despite all his knowledge, the father can see nothing, whereas the ignorant young boy can see far away simply because his point of view is different. He has climbed very high, whereas his father has stayed at ground level.

This is only an analogy, but it will help you understand that, though it is useful to have intellectual faculties and knowledge, the point of view is even more important. You get completely different results if you observe the universe from the earth's point of view or from the sun's point of view. Everybody says, "The sun rises...

the sun sets," and this is true, but it is also false. It is true from the earth's point of view, but it is false from the solar, heliocentric point of view. Everybody looks at life from the earthly point of view and clearly from this angle, they are right. They say, "To live you must eat, earn money and enjoy yourself...." However, if you take the solar angle, looking at things from the spiritual, divine point of view, things look quite different. This is my point of view and so I am able to show you the nature of love and sexuality in a quite different way.

At first glance, it is quite difficult to separate sexuality from love. Everything comes from God and all the energy which flows through man has divine origins. However, this energy has different effects according to what it is passing through. Think of electricity. Electricity is an energy which we cannot define, but when it passes through a light bulb it becomes light, although it is not light itself. It becomes warmth in a heater, magnetism when it passes through a magnet and movement when it goes through a fan. In just the same way, there is a cosmic force which alters its character according to the human organs it passes through. When it goes through the brain, it becomes intelligence and reasoning powers; through the solar plexus (or the Hara centre), it becomes sensations and feelings; through the muscular system, it becomes movement, and when it passes through the genital organs, it becomes attraction for the opposite sex. It is the same energy wherever it goes.

Sexual energy comes from very high up, but on passing through the genital organs it arouses sensations, excitement and the desire to get closer to each other. It is quite possible that with all these manifestations there may be absolutely no love. This is what happens with animals. At set periods during the year, they mate. Is it done with love? No, for they often tear each other apart, and with some insects like the praying mantis and certain spiders, the females eat the male. This is not love, but pure sexuality. Love begins when this energy touches other centres in man, such as his heart, his mind, his soul and his spirit at the same time as it touches his genitals. At this moment the attraction and the desire to draw closer to someone become aesthetic and is made full of light by luminous thoughts and feelings. No longer is the goal that of a purely selfish satisfaction where no account is taken of the feelings of the partner.

Love is sexuality which has been enlarged, enlightened and transformed. Love possesses so many levels and manifestations that they cannot even be counted and classified. For example, a man can love a young and pretty woman whilst not being very physically attracted to her: he wants to see her happy, healthy, well-taught, rich and well-placed in society. How do you explain that? His attitude is not one of mere sexuality, but love, and so it is on a higher level. A trace of sexuality does come into this love when you ask the question: why does this man link himself to this particular woman and not another? Why did he not choose an ugly old woman, or a man? On analysis, you discover that there is an element of sexuality.

Sexuality... love... it is just a question of degree. When you no longer stop at a few coarse, physical sensations, but feel the higher degrees of this cosmic force penetrating you, then you are feeling love and you can communicate with heavenly regions. So many people, once they have satisfied their desire, abandon each other and even come to blows! The only thing that matters to them is to get rid of their tension, and if, after a while, this energy builds up once again, they become smiling and tender once more so that they may once again satisfy their animal desires. What kind of love is that?

Of course we have needs and desires; this is normal, especially when we are young. Nature who has foreseen everything, saw that it was necessary for the propagation of the species. If men and women stayed cold towards each other, if they were detached from their feelings and their instincts, that would be the end of humanity. Therefore nature impels people to draw close to each other physically, but love is quite different.

Sexuality is a purely egocentric tendency which impels people to seek their own personal pleasure. This desire for personal satisfaction can lead to the greatest cruelty as the other person can be forgotten, whereas love, true love, thinks first of all of the happiness of the other person. Love is based on the sacrifice of time, energy and money to help the other one to blossom and develop all their capabilities. Spiritual qualities begin at the point where love dominates sexuality, where the lover becomes capable of giving something of himself for the good of the other. If you cannot deprive yourself for someone, then you do not love. When a man leaps on a girl, does he think of the harm he may do her? Not at all. Sometimes he is ready to kill the girl in order to satisfy his desires, and in his actions you can see sexuality clearly, as a purely bestial instinct.

You may say, "Obviously there is nothing divine in that." Agreed, sexuality is divine by origin, but as long as a person does not know how to control himself, the manifestations will clearly not be divine. The good side of sexuality is its work for the continuation of mankind, but if its only aim is pleasure, then it makes a fine mess of things. Nowadays, in the search for pleasure, they have invented the most improbable objects. There is the pill itself, but also a great quantity of products are being sold, which I do not even wish to mention; they have nothing to do with propagation but are created exclusively for pleasure. I will not dwell on this question to discuss whether these things should exist or not. In the present state of humanity, moralists, both secular and religious, have found it both necessary and totally inevitable that these 'aids' should exist, because the lower nature, the animal nature of man, is still so powerful that if it was not allowed to express itself, it would produce even more undesirable happenings. I do not wish to discuss this, but I will merely say that it is a pity that people are not taught the advantages of controlling this energy and of using it for a heavenly goal, for spiritual work, instead of having recourse to all sorts of products so that they can wallow in pleasure.

There is hardly any difference between love and sexuality in their outer manifestations: there are the same gestures, the same hugs and kisses. The difference lies in the direction that these energies take. When you are impelled by sexuality alone, you do not bother at all about the other person, whereas if you love them, the most important thing for you is to make them happy. The difference between sexuality and love is not so much on the physical plane, but on the invisible, psychic and spiritual plane. How are they different? I am just about to reveal it to you.

All those who have studied the question of sexuality, whether they be physiologists, psychiatrists or sexologists, have never discovered what happens on the subtle, etheric and fluidic plane during the sexual act. They know all about stimulations, tensions and emissions; they have even classified them! What they do not know is that when they are dealing with sexuality which is purely physical, biological and egocentric, it produces on the higher planes all sorts of volcanic eruptions which give off thick emanations and coarse forms. These emanations have dull and murky colours; red is the main colour, but it is a dirty red. All these emanations are swallowed up by the earth or by shadowy creatures who are waiting to feast on these vital energies. Creatures at a low level of evolution feed themselves at the expense of lovers. You are amazed, but it is true: lovers give banquets to the invisible world.

In the olden days, kings and princes gave public banquets which lasted several days when-

ever there was a birth, marriage or great victory.
All the beggars, the drunkards and tramps came
to feast on the food which was distributed to
everybody. So you see that the same thing happens on another level and in a form which
science has not yet discovered. When a man and
a woman are attracted to each other, love each
other and unite, they, too, give a public banquet
and this banquet is spread before many creatures. Even if their union remains secret they
receive visitors from the invisible world and,
unfortunately, it is usually the phantoms and
elementals who come to gorge themselves at the
lovers' expense. They absorb everything because
in these exchanges there are very few elements
for the soul, the spirit and the divine side of
things. For this reason, the exchanges that lovers
make very rarely bring them much benefit. In
fact, quite the opposite occurs: they become
even poorer, something shows in their looks, in
their skin colouring, in their movements, and in
their whole way of behaviour, which is not so
alive and luminous. Their love, because it is at
too low a level, attracts creatures of darkness.
Why don't they invite the nature spirits, the angels and all the luminous spirits who also need
to be fed?

When a magus wants to perform a ceremony,
he begins by drawing a circle of protection

around himself. Harmful spirits are there, hovering and menacing, wanting to injure and destroy him, but they cannot enter because the magus is as sheltered in his circle as if he were in a fortified castle. People have never been taught to protect themselves from the creatures of darkness and it is this fact that once led me to say something very daring: the root of all the sufferings of mankind is the low level of love between men and women. Yes, indeed, it is this love that has produced all wars and plagues. People make love like animals, in a stupid, disgusting and hellish way and so they give food and strength to all the spirits who want to harm mankind. If men and women realized this, they would be so sad, so ashamed and disgusted at what they were doing that they would really try to learn how to love. The Kingdom of God will only come on earth when human love is made more spiritual. May those who are enlightened and who have a high ideal in love, know that they can work for the Kingdom of God with this sexual energy. May they love each other, embrace each other, but always with the idea that this love is dedicated to the realization of something divine. If they do this, they will produce such beautiful emanations that the angels themselves will be amazed and in their delighted wonder, will bring all sorts of gifts to the lovers.

So I repeat that, whatever the nature of your love, the gestures you make will always be the same: you have to draw near to the one you love, you have to hug, kiss and caress them. The difference lies not in the gestures, but in what you put into them; that is the important thing. People say, "Aha, I saw so-and-so kissing someone!" and they condemn him. Heaven is not concerned with the kiss but with what has been put into that kiss; if something pure and beautiful was given, Heaven will reward him. He may be condemned on earth by ignorant people, but he is rewarded by Heaven.

If you put eternal life, purity and light into your love and the one you love grows, progresses and blossoms because of your love, then that is real love, because real love makes everything better. But if you love someone and he begins to go downhill, you should ask yourself a few questions about the quality of your relationship. "What have I done? Once he was splendid but now he is a wreck. I have ruined this person." You have nothing to be very proud of and you will have to find how you can repair all your mistakes.

Your love must make people grow. You can only be proud and happy when you see that someone is growing and blossoming thanks to your love; then you can thank Heaven that you were able to help and protect them. In general, however, most people are not concerned with these things; they come to me saying, "But I really love this person...!" "Yes," I answer, "I know you do, but you love them as you love a chicken which you pop into a cooking pot: you love them, you eat them up and that's the end of that." Oh no, love never devours or damages people. You see, love, as I know it, is a very different thing from the image that most people, especially the unenlightened young, have created for themselves.

People do not know how to love and then, in justification, they say to me, "Oh Master, you do not know how terrible human nature is!" Fine, I see, I do not know human nature! However, I reply that just as they have made their nature unruly, so they can also become wise and make it noble. As they have not made many efforts in the past they inevitably have a very difficult nature to deal with now. This is how it has to be explained: it is their fault and no excuses can justify them. Many decide to stop making efforts because it is impossible, so they say, for them to change. It certainly is possible. Moreover, when you come up against great difficulties, you must say, "The Master told us about this love and I want to get to know it." Why do you always object that the reality of things is different from what I present to you? This word 'reality' is always thrown up to excuse everything; but there are realities and realities.

I do not deny that sexuality is a reality, but why stop at such a low, coarse reality? There are other levels of reality which are just as real, but much finer; those who have reached these levels and live this reality would not give it up, or go back, for anything in the world. The tragedy is that other people cannot be convinced in any way to expand, or raise, their level of love; they ignore all the great saving truths and keep going down to the animal level with the inevitable results of becoming unbalanced and tormented. Predictably, their love can only be wonderful for a few minutes and after that it becomes dust and ashes. They say, "That was so beautiful!" Yes, it was, but it isn't anymore; it did not last and the gold has become lead. Heavenly love, however, always stays pure gold and nothing can tarnish it.

Man has inherited a past that he must fight against; for thousands of years mankind has made love according to a certain pattern which has become recorded in our cells and it is very difficult to erase this pattern. Just because you cannot change yourself from one day to the next does not mean that you should doubt what the great Masters say. If you cannot change yourself, you have proved that you are weak or deformed, but not that the Initiates have misled you. As long as you have lower tendencies, you will be forced to satisfy them, but that does not hinder you from believing that an improvement is possible. When you have developed other tendencies, sublime and divine ones, you will swim in the ocean of cosmic love. Until then you would only have sipped a few scattered drops which you found here and there, mixed in with disappointment and misery, but now you plunge into the cosmic ocean and you drink your fill. No longer need you go and steal a few drops of love from others.

I know that what I am saying will be incomprehensible to some. May they do what they can in the hope that in a few incarnations they will be able to transform their love. There is no point in killing yourself! Those who have already worked on love in other incarnations find it much easier to be satisfied with very little on the physical plane and even free themselves completely so that they can taste love on the spiritual plane.

Obviously, people who are capable of this are very rare. How many monks and nuns have made vows of celibacy without knowing what they were promising! They were very young, they did not know themselves, they did not know human nature and one day when their instincts and passions awoke, they were overwhelmed. What tragedies these men and women suffered! It would have been better to have married and had children than to have tortured themselves in a convent, calling themselves the bride of Jesus whilst all the time their imagination was committing adultery. It would have been better to have left the convent altogether if that was their attitude. The Lord is much more liberal than that; He has never demanded that people should dedicate themselves totally to Him if they are going to suffer torments. He prefers that one should do good by having a wife (or a husband) and children rather than living an unbalanced, chaotic life full of unsatisfied desires which disturb the atmosphere for everybody.

Many, many saints were tormented all their lives by the sexual force and only found peace right at the very end. Saint Theresa of Avila was very passionate. People have no idea how Saint Theresa of the Infant Jesus lived, nor what temptations she had to overcome. She was not at all as she is presented nowadays, a sweet little girl with a tender, delicate face. No, her nature was strong and powerful. I admire her greatly, I love her, and I do not approve of the way people think they improve on her situation by presenting it in this inaccurate manner.

II

Many saints, both men and women, were highly passionate to the very end of their lives and that was no bad thing at all. In fact, it was quite the opposite, as those who know how to use the sexual force are the richest and the most privileged of people. This force is a blessing; yet there have been many devoted believers who have wished to commit suicide because they felt this passion within them and thought they must be damned because of it. They did not understand at all how things are and, unfortunately, the church has done nothing to explain the situation. However, things are seen quite differently from an Initiatic point of view. The sexual force is a gift from God, it is we who must learn how to use it. Countries which have great deposits of coal or oil under their soil have become immensely rich because they make use of their resources. Those who do not know how to use them, burn them. In just the same way, the sexual force is an energy which man must learn to use so that he can turn on the lights, light the fires, and set all the engines within him in motion.

But people are so far from understanding this that when they see that a young girl or boy has a lot of this energy, they are quick to reproach them. They seem to think that young people should feel nothing, that they should behave as though they were dead! So many adults think this and instead of helping a youngster, they try to destroy him and thwart him. Nobody says, "Well done, lad! You are so lucky to have this wealth. The only thing you have to know is that if you are not intelligent, this very wealth will be the cause of great misery." This is what one should say to him, but instead of that, people complain and criticize his energy and rejoice when they see a frigid young man. What on earth can he do with his frigidity? Nothing at all! I, too, was brought up in this way, and it was even worse then than now. If you had any idea how we were brought up in Bulgaria at the beginning of the century! That is why I thank Heaven that I had the light of this Teaching.

So now, if there are any young girls and boys who have come to hear me today for the first time, I will add a few more words to help them. You may perhaps think that I spend too much time talking about objectionable things.... My goodness, this is nothing at all! If you only knew what the youth of today is learning and hearing, what they are talking about and what they are doing, you would be astounded. Little ones of twelve and thirteen tell each other such stories! What I am saying is nothing to what they say.

One day a young girl came to see me; she was pretty, attractive and well brought up. She told me that she was very unhappy because she was obsessed by an image : wherever she looked, at flowers, fruit, objects, even on the ceiling, she saw the image of the male sexual organ. As she was a believer, a good Catholic, she thought she had fallen into sin and was utterly lost.

As she told me this, I began to laugh. She looked at me with an astonished expression and I said, "Now then, will you allow me to explain things to you and show you a way out of your problem?" "Oh yes, please, yes!" she said. This is how I explained it to her. "There is nothing seriously wrong or harmful in what you have told me. It is perfectly natural and normal. Everybody experiences the same thing to a greater or lesser degree. There is no need at all for despair. Nature's task is to make sure that the human race continues and so she creates these pictures in the minds of men and women. However, you must learn how to react and how

to make use of these pictures, because if you
don't, you will always be in the state you are in
now. This is what you must do. When you see
this image on a fruit or any object, don't get upset, look at it calmly. But do not stay looking too
long as certain desires may be awoken and then,
to soothe yourself, you may turn to certain actions and so on and so forth.... To avoid this, become a philosopher: start thinking about the
Cosmic Intelligence which presided over the formation of these organs. Turn these thoughts
over in your mind, and as you meditate on
them, you will be so filled with wonder at the
sublimity which created such perfection that you
will have forgotten the temptation they brought.
If, however, you weigh yourself down with guilt,
you will never get rid of your problem. Think of
this image as the spring-board which can propel
you right up to the source. How could you ever
get up to your goal on high without a spring-
board? Don't forget that you should only take
the image as an impulse; don't contemplate it
for a long time or you will get hopelessly entan-
gled. Make use of it, don't dwell on it. Unfortunately, people do not know how to go beyond
the world of form to one of reflection and wonder. They do not realize that it is precisely this
wonderment which will save them. If you say,
'But what on earth's happening to me? It is hor-

rific and disgusting!' you are done for. Replace your old conceptions and never again say, 'Oh! it's horrific!' but say, 'How beautiful! How magnificent! What intelligence! How did Nature know how to make such an extraordinary thing?' and then in this state of wonder you will once again find your balance and your peace!'' The young girl went away happy after I had said all this to her.

The Lord knew what He was doing and He did it well, so why should you want to mutilate His creations? Some people behave towards sexuality as if the Lord had made a mistake and it is this attitude which is serious and must be punished. We ought to stand in admiration in front of all God's creation because He knows why He created it that way! It is not up to us to criticize it. People have been taught the most extraordinary philosophy! You may say that the intention is to keep people pure and chaste. Yet it is exactly this attitude which drives them to break all the laws of purity; the more things are presented to them as works of the Devil, the more it encourages them to go and experiment!

Do you really believe that by condemning everything to do with sex as ugly and disgusting everybody will stop being interested in it and will leave it alone? Why is it then that the majority of people who find it so disgusting, wallow day and night in this filth? It does not stop them at all. In fact, it acts in quite the opposite way. Baudelaire even said that it is precisely this feeling of committing a crime which gives one the greatest sensation of pleasure, and that pleasure increases when you know that what you are doing is forbidden and unlawful. This may be true, or it may be false, I do not wish to argue about it, but I mention it to point out that denigrating sex is no answer, whereas thinking about it positively will help you.

The only solution to the problem of sexuality lies in the way men and women regard it. The cause of all disorders and excesses is that men and women have never learnt how to esteem each other. If a man thinks of a woman as a female, or as a Messalina, or as an object of pleasure, he has already determined his behaviour towards her and will have to give way to all his passionate tendencies. If he regards her as a divinity, his behaviour is completely transformed.

Jesus said, "Let it be to you according to your faith." Things do indeed change their nature according to the way you look at them. Man must learn this magic law. You think you can change the type of your love without changing the way that you think about the one you love, but I assure you, it is quite impossible. It is very difficult to change the ways you express love, but if you change the way you think about someone, this works on you, on your feelings, your tendencies and so finally, on the way you show your love. This is what I do: I regard all women as divinities. You say, "My dear old chap, you have no idea! If you only knew what women are!..." Do you really think that I do not know? I do not want to dwell either on what they are or on what they might be, because my way of thinking helps me, and so I do it for myself. If you think that I don't know what women are! I have all possible reasons for seeing them as the most revolting of beings, but that attitude does nothing for me. I want women to be divinities for me, because when I regard them as divinities, I get the benefit. If you only knew what I then feel and discover! There is a whole philosophy in my way of looking at things.

Some years ago a doctor came to see me, a fat old doctor with a pot belly; he began to talk to me about women. Do you know what he said? He said, "Women are nothing but vaginas." I was dumbfounded. Tell me, what is the use of such unpoetic conceptions? Of course, it is partly true: one cannot deny that people possess intestines and all sorts of organs which are not particularly aesthetic. However, should we see man as no more than his intestines and his basic functions? People get everything wrong.

Man has to have a physical body with organs adapted to various functions, but he is far from being merely what he appears to be. You cannot reduce men and women to being mere organs; they are beings who think and feel and have a soul and a spirit.

What kind of joy can a man have when he thinks that a woman is nothing more than an organ? All his psychic life is spoilt. That doctor was no real psychologist; he had not studied how our thoughts can affect our inner life. Whereas the discovery of how everything I think affects me is something that really fascinates me. I prefer to think that women are divinities. You say, "But it is not true!" Yes, you may well be right, but I am not interested in your 'good sense,' and your 'truth' is the most pernicious of lies. I live in illusions and lies – supposing that they are illusions and lies – and I am the happiest of mortals. I regard all women as divinities, as an aspect of the Divine Mother, and you can have no idea of the happiness I feel, of the joy I experience, just to know that women live on earth! Do you think that I would keep giving lectures to you if I thought in the same way as that doctor? I would not want to see any of you, I would not want to talk to you, I would not want to do anything.

So you see, this attitude affects many things!

You, too, must change your ideas. Both men and women must change their view on each other, or the doors of evolution will stay closed to them; whatever they do, they will make no progress.

You must never forget that man has two natures: the lower, animal nature which I call the personality and the higher, divine nature called the individuality. The disciple in an Initiatic school, who is aware of these two natures, will always be asking himself how he can best feed his own individuality and those of the people he loves. That is what true love is.

Look at the way people go about winning their partners. Whether we are talking about a man or a woman, they both need to be cajoled, complimented and flattered so that their personality is pampered, otherwise you get nowhere. Both sides know how to get what they want by working on the personality of the other, through words, gestures and presents. They have no idea how to stimulate the sublime faculties in their beloved, how to awaken all that is ideal, luminous and perfect so that just a word, a smile, a look, is a banquet. They know how to arouse and release everything that will allow them to satisfy their lower desires; you can be sure that they know all about that! Human love, therefore, is only expressed at an animal, instinctive and passionate level; it is extremely rare to find any elements of poetry and wonder in it.

Initiatic Science shows people how they can feed the higher nature of those they love. What I am going to say to you may seem very odd; I wonder whether you will understand me, but I am going to say it to you anyway. Let us imagine a woman who is holding her beloved in her arms: obviously she will be saying, "My dear Andrew" or "Dearest John" or "Darling Whoever-you-are" because it is very important that he hears his name said. When he hears it, his personality rejoices at thinking how very much she loves him, and in this way, she sends all her energies to be swallowed up in his personality. Now let us imagine that these two know about the personality and the individuality, that they have been instructed in Initiatic Science: when the woman embraces her beloved, she will say, "O Heavenly Father!..." and her beloved will be so happy to become a conductor of energies which will go right up to the Heavenly Father Himself! In his turn, he connects himself to the Divine Mother as he embraces his beloved and so his energies go straight up to Heaven.

Men and women should connect themselves to the source which is God Himself instead of limiting their exchanges to lower levels where they can give and take all sorts of putrefying and fermenting rubbish. They should connect themselves to this source of perfection, not to an imperfect and limited person like themselves. You have heard men say, "Sweetheart, I will make you happy." One look at this weak, ignorant and unhappy specimen and you know that he could not make someone else happy. There is only one way lovers will find a pure, incorruptible love which will satisfy them, a love which will enlighten, make them strong, youthful and bring them happiness; this is by committing each other to the Heavenly Father and the Divine Mother with their inexhaustible supplies. You, too, must learn ceaselessly to create and maintain this link with divine love. Everything you do must be reasonable, purified, consecrated and sanctified in the service of a noble idea, that of the Kingdom of God and His Justice.

People do not know this truth. They only work for their own personality and that of others; as personality has subterranean roots, it leads them down to the depths. It is so difficult to encourage people to change their point of view. They have their old habits and they keep reinforcing them; they always satisfy their personality and they give nothing to their poor, starving individuality.

Unfortunately, personality which receives so

much every day that it ought to be satiated, is never grateful. You want proof of this? Think of a woman who gives everything to the man she loves, everything, yet he forgets her and goes off with other women. Why? Because she only satisfied his sexual desires. She does nothing for the sublime in him, she does not give anything to his higher nature which would never forget the good that has been done to it and would be eternally grateful. The poor woman complains, "I gave him everything and now look how he has treated me!" Yes indeed, because she only fed the nature which is never grateful.

Once you really understand the concept of these two natures, you will find it much easier to resolve your sexual problems. Those who allow themselves to follow all their selfish whims will not be able to control their sexuality; it will seem as though their organs will function quite separately from them and they will not be able to slow down or stop themselves. Helpless, they will watch other forces taking over, whilst they are only there as observers. With spiritual love, on the other hand, you will notice that it is you, the real you, your soul, spirit and individuality which is in charge and which grows. It may only be a look, a presence, a perfume which makes you happy and elated but you feel that it is your real self, your higher nature which has eaten, drunk and inhaled, not all sorts of foreign entities that have been making use of you.

I am giving you the light of truth on this subject; believe me, I invent nothing. Love is the greatest mystery that exists; people know nothing about it, yet go on practising it without thought or understanding. They flounder about in unhappy muddles all the time, and until this question of love is understood and resolved, they will never get out of their misery, no matter what amazing discoveries science may make. Here then is the point of view which Heaven has given me which allows me to see the whole question very clearly.

3

THE SEXUAL FORCE IS ESSENTIAL
FOR LIFE ON EARTH

Young children start by crawling on all fours on the ground; everything they see they want to touch and put into their mouths. Little by little, as they grow up, their hearts awaken. A boy finds that girls become very important to him, he falls in love and wants to have a home so that he can people the world with his achievements and his children. Much later, when he has spent all his energy and seen that he has grown old without achieving all his dreams, he changes; he loses interest in the world and begins to think of the other world. The man who once thought only of eating, drinking, having children and making money, as if he was never going to have to leave this world, has now become so uninterested, cold, impersonal, tired and bored that he prepares to give up everything and die. What has happened? The cause of his change is due, quite simply, to a weakening of his sexual instinct.

I am going to show you how the sexual force determines a man's philosophy. With this force, he is happy to live here and now, but when it has left him, he thinks only of death. That is why certain Initiates in the past who knew all these things, what their causes and consequences were, taught their disciples that if they wanted to free themselves from the limitations and sufferings of this earth for a blissful world of light, they must suppress all manifestations of their sexual force. They were told to flee from all desires and lusts, and to avoid the opposite sex, lest they be caught in their snares.

We can therefore say that the sexual force is at the root of all the different tendencies in philosophies and religions. The attitude that people choose to adopt towards the attraction between the sexes determines their philosophy: whether to suppress the sexual force, or to give it an outlet. Of course there are many other philosophies but all of them can be fitted into one or other of these two categories.

If you do not wish to go on suffering here on earth, if you want to enter eternity and become immortal, you must not consider having children because they create bonds which keep you earthbound. You are linked to the father or mother of your children, you are physically linked to your children who are flesh of your flesh, blood of your blood, and you are also linked psychically to them. The Buddhist philosophy teaches that even when a man has passed over to the other side, thinking he has left everything and can now be free, he finds that he is still connected to his children and his parents. He cannot, therefore, leave the lower regions of the astral plane and stays for a while very close to people, especially the members of his family; he watches them, takes part in their lives and even feeds himself through them. According to this philosophy, if you want to be free, you must neither marry nor have children, because those who have started a family to carry on their name are attracted by that name, by the 'family firm,' you could say, and so they have to keep coming back to earth as the family down there keeps calling them with their thoughts.

All connections that men have with earth hinder them from staying in heavenly regions, so those who really do not want these links live an ascetic life. Clearly their philosophy is valid, for it is based on Initiatic truths, but it is quite another question to know whether it is useful and well adapted to the present day. It may indeed be that it is no longer viable. These are questions that need to be answered. The sexual force binds people to the earth without enlightening them or connecting them to the sublime regions on high; whereas the wisdom which enlightens Initiates can bring them closer to these sublime regions, but then they no longer wish to live on earth. Those who want to suppress completely this force which God has given them think only of death and of abandoning everything. The sexual force is essential for life and is the one thing which can make you love life. Therefore you must never suppress this force; all those who have suppressed it have committed a most serious mistake. Their justification is a desire for nirvâna, but they desire nirvâna so passively and feebly one wonders if they will ever get there. Love must participate if we are to reach nirvâna.

The man who is really enlightened connects himself to Heaven and at the same time he looks after his resources, dedicating his sexual energy to the realization of the Kingdom of God on earth. In this way he has the best of both worlds: the more intensely he lives his life, the more he merges and becomes one with his Creator and with Heaven itself; the closer his bond with Heaven, the more work he will be able to do for the world. This is the only perfect solution: at one and the same time, he lives for Heaven and he works on earth. Otherwise, life is without rhyme or reason.

Unfortunately, people have never been able to understand this and they are always trying to choose either one or the other. They are either completely materialistic or completely... we can't say 'spiritualized' because there is nothing spiritual about wanting to die. In any case, those who have chosen suppression of the sexual force to avoid future incarnations will nevertheless be made to reincarnate, and not just once, but many times! Yes, they will come back to learn that they must not suppress it. Heaven will say to them, "Oh you ignoramuses! God in all His wisdom created this force millions of years ago. Why have you despised it?" and they will be sent back to earth.

Puritans and certain mystics preached a morality which did not really correspond to the truth and which led in the end to all the anomalies which psychoanalysts are having to deal with today. If you build a dam on a river without a headrace, the water will overflow and flood everything. Dams won't stop the water from flowing. The same thing is true of human beings: put barriers across your mounting energies, the tension accumulates in your subconscious, and then a moment comes when everything is swept away. Yes, indeed, if you do not know human nature, you court disaster. You must never block your energies, but prepare channels so that they can flow and irrigate your land, just as the ancient Egyptians dug canals so that the Nile could irrigate their country.

I am not in favour of either debauchery or

puritanism. Those who suppress everything are unaware of God's reason for creating both men and women. When I was in Greece, I visited all the monasteries on Mount Athos and spoke with the monks who lived there. Though I very much admired their works of art, I derived a great feeling of sadness and boredom from the place. The monks live according to totally misguided conceptions, the main one being that the feminine principle is both harmful and diabolical. They have gone so far in their rejection of the feminine principle that not only is no woman allowed to set foot on the island but also they are not allowed to have a goat on the island because it is a female animal. Do you really think the Good Lord was capable of inspiring such a philosophy?

I repeat, I am neither for a puritanical philosophy nor for debauchery, and so I bring you a third solution : connect yourself, spirit and soul, to the source of love and, at the same time, get on with your work here on earth. One day you will realize that it is the best solution, to have both Heaven and earth at the same time.

I do not know if you are convinced by my explanations, but perhaps sometime in the future you will accept them, when you see that I have found the solution to problems which others have not solved because either they could not, or dared not, unite the two : either they gave free rein to the sexual force and ended in debauchery or they suppressed it completely and became eunuchs. When you suppress this force, you annihilate yourself; life loses its savour and you become sour and bad tempered. What can one expect from a eunuch? Do you think he will compose symphonies or write poems? A eunuch is unable to create; for him it is over and done with, he might as well be dead!

4

PLEASURE

I

Do Not Seek Pleasure
for It Will Impoverish You

Nowadays, young people demand sexual freedom thinking that that is the road to happiness and fulfilment. It is very easy to get hold of the contraceptive pill and they are glad that they no longer need to think first in order to control themselves or their situation. "No, no, let's shut our eyes and get on with it!" This notorious pill is having more and more success throughout the world. When it was first produced, it was marketed to control the population, but then all sorts of other reasons were added, the main one being the desire to have pleasure without any complications. I ask you, do girls of thirteen really need the pill? Yet they are letting them use it at this age and I have learnt that in certain schools it is the teachers themselves who hand the pill out to their pupils, yes, the teachers!

When young people are allowed to rush into experiences in an unknown area, they are opening the door to all sorts of physical and psychic

disturbances. They do not know that their experiments will have catastrophic results in the
long term which will make them ill and unbalanced. An essential fact has not been understood
both by those who are for, and those who are
against, the pill. Those in favour know that people are weak and so they support this weakness;
those against do it out of hypocrisy, citing old
moral attitudes which they themselves are the
first to ignore in their own private lives.

Science thinks it has done a great service to
mankind by inventing the pill, whereas by al-
lowing people to go to extremes, it is actually encouraging them to become weak, sensual and ill.
What benefits! Before the pill, girls and boys at
least had to think, to control themselves a little
(not from reasons of morality or purity, I agree,
but out of fear of undesirable consequences
which might occur), whereas now they do not
have to bother about controlling themselves at
all, they can let themselves go.

Let me give you an analogy. You all know
how ships operated in the past. Down below
there were stokers who shovelled coal into
boilers and it was their work which made the
ship move forward: but they themselves could
not see which direction the ship was taking, that
was the work of a captain up on the bridge who
could steer and give commands, but had nothing

to do with making the ship move. The emotions, feelings and instincts of man are like the fuel put into the boiler to make the ship move forward. If there is no one of clear good sense on the bridge at the helm, the ship will founder and break into pieces.

During a cruise in the Arctic Ocean a lady asked the captain, "What will happen if our boat meets an iceberg?" "Oh," replied the captain, "the iceberg will stay right on course, ma'am." And the boat? He didn't mention the ship for obvious reasons, just as there is not much we can say if a man's ship lurches into an iceberg. Of course, we are speaking symbolically: the 'captain' here is the head and the 'stokers' are everywhere in the body, in the stomach, the sexual organs, the abdomen.... So I say to the young: if you follow your wishes, desires and whims, it is absolutely certain that you will fall flat on your face, because these impulses of yours are quite blind.

Recently I heard a pretty girl say on television, "I satisfy all my desires without any complexes." There you are, she is free from any 'complexes' or should it be free from wisdom, self-control and discernment? It appears that these are 'complexes,' and 'complexes' are bad for you and so you must get rid of them. So that you can go where? So that you can find what?

So that you can do what? Anything under the
sun!

I would like to put a question to all these
boys and girls who know exactly what they
should be doing. "When you are working in a
factory, or when you are driving a car, aren't
you in charge of your machine? And when you
are cooking something, don't you regulate the
temperature and measure the sugar and all of the
other ingredients?" Well then, realize that the
same thing goes on inside you; if you are not
careful and if you do not control all your inner
motors and machinery, watch out for the results!

Today, young people have only one idea,
and that is that they should leap over all the
moral barriers that the Initiates of the past put
up to keep people from living in the midst of disorder and overwhelming passion. So many daz-
zling civilisations have vanished, ravaged by
moral and physical illness because they gave
themselves up to debauchery and orgiastic cults!
Now the modern generation wants to be free of
all taboos, to break all the rules. This movement
towards the greatest amount of pleasure has
grown so powerful that one wonders what will
be able to stop it. In fact, only the light of an Initiatic teaching can hold humanity back from this
dizzying fall. This light will make them see that

by giving themselves over to pleasure they are
sacrificing their most precious energies. To keep
the fire going they have to throw in all their resources, and all their furniture, right down to the
table and chairs. Sexual pleasure is a furnace
which they have to feed with their very substance; it cannot be satisfied with their neigh-
bours' fuel or with wood from the forest; it feeds
on their own reserves and their own fuel.... To
keep it flaming away each day at the same feverish pitch of excitement with constant volcanic
eruptions means they have to burn their quintessence, which is our most precious possession.
Without realizing it, each eruption takes away a
little of their beauty, their intelligence, their
strength, and then when all is spent, they end up
ugly, stupid and ill.

If only there was a pair of scales in which you
could put on one side what you had gained in
tasting all these sensual pleasures and on the
other side what you had lost by giving way, you
would see that you had lost practically everything and gained practically nothing. It is really
not worthwhile sacrificing everything for nothing. As you never think that feelings can be
short-lived and forgotten (the food you ate yes-
terday cannot nourish you today), you are preparing a life of poverty for your future. If you
make an effort to refuse, you suffer for a mo-

ment, but you are preparing a magnificent future for yourself. You may give up a few sensations, but you are gaining your future. Those who do not think say, "I am happy, I feel good!" It may be true, but they will have no future ahead of them. This philosophy is summed up by the drunkard: his pleasure lies in drinking, because wine makes him happy, he drinks wine. Yes, he's happy, but if he keeps on drinking, how are his boss, his family and his friends going to react? The feeling he has is pleasant, but not for long. His future is in the gutter.

Do you remember the story in the Bible where Esau sold his birthright to his brother Jacob for a bowl of lentils? For a sensation, for pleasure, he sacrificed his birthright and Jacob profited. This story has never been properly interpreted. Most people are very good at giving up the most precious thing they own in exchange for a little pleasure; that's the one thing they know how to do really well, it's extraordinary! When will they begin to understand that they have to deprive themselves of certain pleasures if they are to obtain others infinitely more precious?

Morality is no longer respected because people do not realize that originally it was based on real knowledge. Blindly, stupidly, people follow all their whims without realizing that they are galloping towards utter ruin. Once you destroy the dams and the dykes, there will be an inevitable and devastating flood. So that is why I tell the young, "My children, you must learn to discern where each one of your desires is going to lead you. If you feel that you have become poorer, weaker and unhappy, you know that you are on the wrong track. Choose another one! Never choose a path for the simple reason that it is pleasant and sweet tasting, because that way you will ruin yourself spiritually and physically as well."

II

Replace Pleasure with Work

Most people seek pleasure, they are addicted to it as if there was nothing better. That is where they are wrong. I will prove it to you by giving you a little example which comes from man's prehistory.

Matches and lighters are recent inventions and our distant ancestors had to light fires by other methods. One of these was done by rubbing two sticks of wood together; this friction first produced heat, and then after some time, all of a sudden a flame sprang up and there was light. You all know this phenomenon, but have you thought of looking for the psychological truths that lie behind this physical, mechanical phenomenon? You notice facts and leave it at that, without noticing and interpreting the inner meaning.

Let us see what we can learn from this example. We take two pieces of wood, rub them against each other, this movement becomes heat and the heat is transformed into light. Movement, heat and light are the three sides of the triangle which I have often spoken about as representing the human being. Movement is associated with willpower, activity and strength; heat is associated with the heart, with feelings and with love; and light corresponds to intelligence, thought and wisdom. So let us look at this process in the realm of love. What do people do when they make love? Symbolically speaking, we could say that like the two pieces of wood, lovers rub against each other to produce warmth, or a feeling of pleasure. That's fine, but why do they stop there? Why is there no light? Why are their minds not illuminated? Love ought to bring them light, so that they can understand all the mysteries of the universe, they ought to become crystal clear and clairvoyant! But no, they merely grow more stupid.

Movement and warmth is all that people understand of love at the moment. They stop halfway along the path, before they reach light itself. Looking for thrills absorbs all their energies and stops the light blazing forth. So then, it is totally clear and simple: don't stop en route, but go up to the heights, right to light itself. Of course there are many things to see along the path, and some of them are most seductive, but they are only tinsel snares for the unwary; if you let them divert you, you will never achieve your goal. I say to lovers: your movements have produced heat and that is fine, but now you must go on to produce light, as light should be the goal of every action.

Nearly everybody stops on their journey because that is where they find all that is attractive and glittering... but this is also the point where they meet the sirens who tear them apart. Do you remember the legend of Ulysses? Ulysses was a wise man who knew that he was going to encounter the sirens; these creatures would try to capture him by their singing so that they could then devour him, so he stopped the ears of his fellow sailors with wax. He knew that they would not be able to resist the sirens' song if they heard it. As for himself, he did not block his own ears because he wanted to hear their song, but he said to his companions, "Tie me to the mast. If I command you by signs to release me, bind me even more tightly!" As the boat approached the island, the sound of their voices made Ulysses lose his head in his desire to join the sirens. He shouted to his sailors to untie him. He threatened them with death if they did not free him, but they, faithful to their charge, tightened his bonds. You see, the sirens are halfway along the path and you must not stop for them. Nobody questions that there are delightful and seductive things en route, but they must not stop you.

In Wagner's opera "Parsifal," Parsifal comes to a meadow where he finds the young flower maidens who try to seduce him, but behind their flowers lurk snakes. This story (like many others in world literature) conceals great occult truths. Ulysses and Parsifal are both symbols of the Initiate who meets temptations on his path; if the Initiate stops, he will lose his life. He must go on, right to the summit, and once he has got there, he is given everything: rest, food, beauty and love.

Here is another way of seeing this truth. You have been given a job to do which entails your going through a forest, full of all sorts of fruit and flowers, in particular, wild strawberries.... You dart hither and thither, picking them and unaware that you are wasting a lot of time; they are all so very pretty and delicious. Meanwhile night has fallen; you cannot see where you are going, you are lost; all around you you hear the cries of wild animals, the cracking of branches, and you are terrified. Yes, that is what happens to disciples who stop on their path because of pretty strawberries! You protest that you have never stopped for strawberries? That may be true, but strawberries can also be pretty girls or several drinks at the bistro. I am speaking symbolically, you understand. Little strawberries can also be big strawberries!

So pleasure is exactly this: strawberries, sirens and flower maidens, and if you fall for it, you will be eaten. By whom? By elementals, phantoms, subterranean spirits and undesirable beings, who see that you are giving a banquet, and so they flock to it. I have already explained to you that exchanges between men and women are like banquets which attract the spirits of the invisible world. When lovers are only after their own pleasure, they attract all these lower entities which then feed at the lovers' expense, and cause their downfall.

I could say much about these banquets. When a very rich man gives a reception, he has all sorts of different courses, wines, flowers and the most beautiful of china, silver, linen and crystal glasses. This all costs a great deal and some people have bankrupted themselves by giving such sumptuous receptions. The same thing happens with ignorant lovers; they use up their capital. Unfortunately they do not realize it, they do not notice that they are using up their strength and their fluidic energies. Go and look at them sometime later and you will see they are ruined and all their fine feathers have gone.

When the rich give their big receptions, pickpockets and swindlers mingle with the guests to steal their money, jewels and works of art. In the same way, whilst lovers are at their banquet, robbers creep into them, the worst kind of robbers who do not take objects but who take what is in the hearts and minds of the owners of the house. They take their inspiration, they take their ideas, the flights of their minds, the yearnings of their hearts, and all of their plans; once they have been stripped in this way, the unhappy couple no longer have the same enthusiasm, the same longing to know the secrets of the universe. No, now they have other very mundane desires. Yes indeed, you must learn to observe and to use the law of analogy to understand everything that goes on.

My dear brothers and sisters, I am leading you towards truths that the invisible world has revealed to me. I have studied and observed people and I have seen that what I have just told you is absolutely true. Lovers who are driven only by a desire for pleasure allow burglars free entry. They must have a much higher ideal if the light is going to spring forth. There will be banquets and invitations, but instead of attracting all the objectionable beings of the astral plane, the light will invite angels and divinities to rejoice with them. As these heavenly beings leave presents behind them, the lovers will receive a hundred times more than they gave. Instead of being robbed, they will become younger and more full of life, they will have revelations, ecstasies, and flights of inspiration.

People will not find the solution to their sexual problems by wallowing in pleasure. Pleasure is only halfway along the path; if they stay there, they will gradually find that they are becoming bound, that they have lost all their freedom and lightness of heart. A butterfly cannot fly when its wings are soaked with moisture. That's what pleasure is: too much moisture. When I see a man whose wings cannot lift him (symbolically speaking), I do not need to ask him where he has been hiding himself, I know that he has exposed his wings to too much dampness. It is very obvious to me that moisture prevents flight. It takes a long time to dry out in the light. So beware; do not be deceived by pleasure which will stop you mid-way... go right on to the light!

Let me make myself quite clear: I have never said that men and women should not give each other a lot of love. You should indeed love each other all the time, but on a higher, more luminous plane, above the physical, rather than by stimulating each other, satisfying each other and then turning over to snore; you must be conscious of the importance and the sacred quality of the sexual act. However, everyone is in such a hurry, racing to bury themselves in the mire, giving themselves no time to think. Their gestures tend to be feverish and abrupt, their looks are cloudy with sensuality.... The man longs for satisfaction, he wants only to rip apart and devour the woman, who in her stupidity is delighted when she sees him wild with desire! If she were a little more evolved she would be frightened by what she sees and by what lies in store for her, because this look shows he is prepared to take everything, to ruin her, but she likes that, it is what she wants! If the man looked at her with respect and wonder she wouldn't be nearly as happy. She doesn't like it when someone gives her a pure look filled with light, "I can't expect much from that one," she thinks and drops him. Instinctively, a woman likes to feel she is putty in a man's hands, to be beaten and pounded and kneaded... this is what she enjoys, whereas a look full of respect, a heavenly look means nothing at all. There are exceptions, but in general this is so true of women!

You ask, "My goodness, is one never to have pleasure?" Of course, but you must look for a much more subtle, much more spiritual, pleasure. Pleasure, as it is now understood, always turns bitterly poisonous. When you cut a piece of lead, it shines for a while and then it darkens. Pleasure is like lead. If you want your pleasure to be as shining and as resistant as gold, you must make it more noble, by adding another element, the element of thought. You must replace the idea of pleasure with that of work.

A man works when he stops seeking thrills which waste his energies but uses those energies to make other centres function in his brain. Instead of releasing whirlwinds and volcanic eruptions within himself, he keeps his clarity of thought to channel these currents and guide them so that they waken new faculties which will make him a genius, an Initiate, a divinity. That is how he turns heat into light: he replaces pleasure with work and at that moment he experiences real pleasure, a pleasure which, instead of debasing him, uplifts and ennobles him.

Everybody thinks that if you are too clearheaded you lose all pleasure, the more lucid you are, the less pleasure you feel. In fact, thought was given to man so that he could experience real love more fully; without this power to think he would be dominated by his primitive, animal side. Only by letting his thoughts be governed by his intelligence can he control, direct and sublimate his energies. Keep your thoughts lucid when you love, let your mind survey your love, watch over it, controlling and directing the forces. You may not be feeling the pleasure that most people know, a mindless, uncontrollable pleasure that an animal feels with nothing noble and spiritual about it, but thanks to the light, pleasure has been transformed into joy, wonder, rapture and ecstasy. Lead becomes pure gold.

Pleasure is the result of an action that is in harmony with other substances and presences. Therefore if the action is in perfect harmony with the divine world, the pleasure which comes from it is increased and augmented infinitely. At the moment you experience a certain pleasure, but it is of such coarse, low quality and you will have to pay so dearly for it, that it really is not worth it. Of course you must experience pleasure, but it should be such a fine and magnificent pleasure that it will reveal the universe to you, it will make you luminous, beautiful, expressive, powerful and useful! That kind of pleasure is worth the effort and it will not be taken away from you.

Dear brothers and sisters, don't stop along the way. You should try to attain the farthest reaches of pleasure and not stay forever on the same low level; you must climb up higher, right up through the clouds to where you can see the light of the sun. Do not linger below the clouds; have a luminous goal at the end of each endeavor. Whatever you are doing, whether you are eating, or walking, or kissing, make your goal the Light. Do nothing merely for your own pleasure; humanity is disintegrating because everybody is hell-bent on pleasure. You say, "But if we are to feel no pleasure in anything we are doing, life will lose all its meaning." No, because everything works together: as soon as light and warmth are there (by which I mean intelligence and love), pleasure will follow automatically. The quality will be different, the pleasure and the intensity will change. So think about this, meditate on it and never forget that your love should lead you right up to the Light.

5

THE DANGERS OF TANTRIC YOGA

In India and Tibet there is a science of sublimating the sexual force which is called Tantra Yoga. There are many methods involved and I will describe one of them to give you an idea of this science. The yogi works for years studying the subject of love, meditating, fasting and doing breathing exercises. When he is ready, a young woman will be chosen for him. This woman has also been taught and prepared for these practices and the two of them will live together in the same room for four months. The yogi puts himself completely at her service, treating her as a divinity; he regards her as a manifestation of the Divine Mother, but he does not touch her. Then they begin to sleep in the same bed; for four months the woman sleeps on the right side of the man and then for four months on his left, still without touching each other. Finally, when they have acquired complete control, they begin to embrace and even to merge with each other, but

in such great purity that they can be together for
hours without any emission.

Obviously very few people will have any idea
of what this means, because, in general, the min-
ute they feel their sexual desire awaken, they
rush to find an outlet for it. According to tantric
science, to waste this quintessence is to invite
death, whereas its sublimation brings eternal
life. In this way several Initiates have attained
immortality. Oh yes, these are not mere words,
Initiates have become immortal.

You have to be very strong and very pure to
be able to dive into the realm of the subconscious, the ocean of instinct and passion, sensuality and pleasure, without danger. Those who
are capable bring back precious pearls from the
depths, like deep sea divers retrieving the pearl
laden oysters whilst avoiding the danger of sea-
weeds and killer sharks. You must be master of
this formidable force in order to confront it.
However, I am not advising you to try it, I am
merely explaining it.

Once you have been able to go a certain distance into the realm of the superconscience,
once you have tasted the quintessence of God,
the love that fills the universe, you are safe to do
whatever you want; for you, sin is no longer
possible and nothing can contaminate or harm
you in any way. Before reaching that point, it is

better to wait and not explore the depths of your lower nature as very few are capable of transforming and sublimating the things they find into something beautiful and luminous. This work is the real meaning of the phrase 'making both ends meet,' when the top and the bottom, the higher and lower levels are joined. You will be wiped out by the lower world if you explore it too soon before having been able to reach the higher world. You will not be sufficiently protected or armed, you will not have the instruments you need in order to change the crude ore of Hell into gold, into precious stones and pearls.

That is the mystery of evil and of Hell. Only when you have been to the heights can you understand the meaning of the depths of evil. Until then, the problem of evil will remain incomprehensible and insoluble for you. The problem of evil is not solved by reasoning, by scholarly studies, or by reading books; the problem of evil is beyond human comprehension. Actually, evil does not exist. Evil is only evil to weaklings, to the unprepared, to those who do not know how to use it. For them, evil exists and is a very powerful reality. However, for the sons of God, for the great Masters, evil, so little understood and so often preached against, is a priceless substance essential to their work.

When I was in India, I met certain yogis called siddhas, who consider nothing dirty or impure; they eat rubbish, animal entrails, excrement, anything, as an exercise in transformation. They believe that by learning to transform everything they will be able to develop extraordinary magical powers; they really do obtain these powers, I was able to verify that. However, in my opinion, it is not necessary to use quite such bizarre and unaesthetic methods.

To return to tantric techniques, I am not very much in favour of them, particularly if they are practised by Westerners. The Universal White Brotherhood has other methods for the sublimation of the sexual energy and when you know them you will see that this Teaching far surpasses both those Christian traditions of so-called purity and chastity which turned men into eunuchs as well as those doctrines under the heading of Tantrism, that led to all kinds of sexual excesses. In the last century, there was an occultist, an Englishman by the name of Aleister Crowley, who wished to have the same experiences as the Tibetans. He sank so low as to experiment with black magic, with the result that several women went mad during his experiments. He had undeniable powers, but at what a price he obtained them!

For this reason I do not advise you to venture into this kind of experience for you will not come out unscathed. In order to practice Tantric Yoga, you must be very sure, very expert, very much in control, and even then it is extremely dangerous. The best solution, the one that will keep you out of danger, is distance, distance mixed with homeopathic doses, that is, to be content with a look, a smile, a handshake, a few words. If you want to draw closer and unite, then it is much more difficult: once you are in the fire, you will be unable to control yourself, you will no longer be master of your energies and it is totally useless to start talking about Tantric Yoga then!

6

LOVE WITHOUT WAITING TO BE LOVED

As I have told you, I know all the methods of Tantra Yoga, but I have gone even farther. I find it unnecessary to do all the things in the books on Tantric Yoga, to sublimate my sexual energy, and to obtain perfect control. I favour another Tantra Yoga which surpasses these others.

One of the methods is to learn to love without waiting to be loved; in this way you are wonderfully free. Unfortunately, people are not interested in liberty; they prefer chains which weigh them down. Liberty bores them and they do not know what to do with it! At least when you are buffeted and compelled, you have something to think about! You can suffer and weep! Only the great Masters have solved this problem; instead of wondering if they are loved they just behave like the sun, endlessly pouring down their love on everything. They are unconcerned where this love goes, whether it touches anyone or everyone. The only thing they care about is that this divine energy should pass through them and that they should feel full of wonder and inspiration.

Many people have come to me with this problem: should they go on loving a man or woman who is no longer living rightly? Love is a way of helping as it always has beneficial effects in the higher regions of others. On the other hand, it is preferable not to dedicate too much time and energy to someone who is not worth it. The only thing that matters is to love; if it is not one particular man or woman, let it be other people, let it be the whole world, just so long as the river keeps on flowing. It does not matter where it flows; but flow it must. You will suffer if the river stops flowing, your inspiration will be gone, your wings clipped. Do not wait to start loving again until you have found another attractive little face, as that will be the beginning of the end once more!

You must realize that love, true love, is above both sexual attraction and feeling. Love is a state of consciousness, whereas attraction is a phenomenon which can be felt only for some things as it depends on purely physical elements such as wavelengths, vibrations and fluids. Feelings are of a higher order than attraction because they can be inspired by intellectual, spiritual and moral factors, yet they too are changeable;

one day you love, the next you don't. People are not at all consistent in their feelings towards their wives, children, lovers, mistresses and friends, but love, lived as a state of consciousness, is above all circumstances and personalities. A being who is so purified, so developed in willpower, that he can lift himself, whatever he is doing, to the sublime regions of divine love will feel this love and give it to help everyone he meets.

If you are to reach this level of consciousness, you have to gain control so that nothing happens without your decision. You want to kiss a girl.... Yes, you can do it, but only when you have consciously decided it and you do not have that right before you have spent many years purifying yourself. If you leave any marks or stains on her, the invisible world will condemn you. You have no right to kiss someone, or have physical exchanges with them until you have arrived at the level where you will leave only those elements which will go on working for their good, until you give life and light.

Your love will become unchangeable the day you feel love as a state of consciousness. You are so far from being able to understand this idea! Humanity is so changeable: one moment you love people and objects and jobs, and the next, you don't. Stability is not very common. Even you, dear brothers and sisters, come to the sunrise and are uplifted and amazed, but after the first few days, it becomes automatic and you have lost your first enthusiasm. To avoid this, do everything as if it were for the first time: go each morning to meet the sun as if it were for the very first time... see your husband and wife each day as if for the very first time. Yes, even after fifty years, feel as full of wonder as on the first day! You say that it is not possible. If you see love as a feeling or an attraction, it is not possible, but if you have learnt to live love as a state of consciousness, then it is possible.

Many artists have chosen to have affairs in order to stimulate their inspiration. Unfortunately, this sensual, egotistic, capricious love, which is indeed the source of some inspiration, is also the main source of the greatest disorders. Love is like wine: it makes you drunk, but the drunkenness that you find in these lower regions leads to the same physical and moral decay as the abuse of alcohol. The greatest victory is to know how to love, as true love never destroys you.

You must understand that the only solution to the problems of love is Love itself. Many have come to me to complain about certain illnesses or imbalances and I say to them, "Why did you stop loving? These troubles came because you restrained your love. Love is a mighty torrent, but as you did not know this and how to deal with it, you repressed it, and the repression led to devastation as the torrent swept away all barriers. If you want to save yourself from these miseries, you must love, day and night, love everything... and then you will be so busy that there will be no time left to be tormented. The more you shut yourself off, the more you are miserly with love, the greater the complications you will experience. My God, if you would only be generous, you would be saved; give your love to everything. I have discovered this secret and this is what I do. Quite clearly people think that I am a little childish and say, "Poor chap, him and his heart...." But that's precisely it! With my heart I have found the secret which you, with all your highly developed intelligence, haven't yet discovered.

Thank Heaven each day for the wonders around you, for the millions of beautiful women and strong, intelligent men you have not yet had the happiness of meeting. Think about them and rejoice! Rejoice that they exist and that one day you might meet them, talk to them, and admire them. My suggestion astonishes you as you are not used to rejoicing over ideas like this. Indeed, it is a very unusual way of thinking, but it is so effective! Try it and see!

You say, "Yes, but this goes against all the laws of morality. If everyone loved everyone, the family would no longer exist." Of course it would, it would be just one big family and that's no bad thing. When I say that men must love all women and women must love all men that does not mean that they should have lots of experiences and be unfaithful to each other. No, they must be faithful, but they must also realize that no one man or woman can give everything and that you yourself cannot give everything to your beloved. So we should live and work together, but love the whole world, smile at the whole world, and leave our partners free to do the same. Go on loving each other, go on being together, but enlarge your concept of love and learn to be happy with subtle joys.

Man will always be faced with the question of love but there will be variations in the way we manifest it. In the future, everyone will learn to love all men and women; there will be no more room in our hearts for selfish, personal and limited elements as we fill our hearts and souls with the immensity of the splendour of Heaven.

7

LOVE IS EVERYWHERE
IN THE UNIVERSE

Ask a man what he loves in a particular woman and he will say that he loves her breasts or her legs, her mouth, her hair or her eyes.... Nature has made use of all these attractive forms with one goal in mind; she wants to make sure that humanity never disappears and so she created beautiful legs and lovely hair which keep on encouraging people to populate the earth. Lovers do not know that what they are really attracted by lies behind the appearance; it is an emanation, a fluid, that acts and when it is missing, they no longer feel attracted. Why is it that the prettiest women with the best figures are not necessarily the most attractive to men? They are admired but they are not the ones to be pursued and wooed. Yet other girls who are not so pretty and well-made have an extraordinary effect on men.

This proves that attraction does not depend entirely on physical beauty, but on another,

spiritual, magical element. That is why the ignorant call love inexplicable. It is, in fact, explica-
ble, for those who know that this vibration, this
fluid, which makes you feel so happy, does not
originate in a man or woman and therefore can
be found at its source. It comes from another region and the Creator Himself distributes it. It is
such a pity that, for the most part, people turn
away from this immense, inexhaustible supply
and go to look for it in men and women where
they can only find a few particles.

It is love we seek, not a particular man or
woman. A man leaves his wife (or a wife her
husband) because he has found love elsewhere
with another woman. If he does not find love
with her, he will go and look for it with a third
woman... or a fourth.... It is love which counts,
love, and not the woman or the man. If it was
the individuals that counted, they would never
leave each other.

In fact, love is everywhere in the universe. It
is an element, an energy, which is distributed
throughout the whole cosmos, and it can be
picked up by people through their skin, their
eyes, ears and brain. A plant revealed to me that
love is everywhere! As I have told you, I get my
information from plants, stones, insects and
birds. One day, in Nice, I saw a plant that was
suspended in the air, it hung in the air, it subsist-

ed on air and didn't need to bury its roots in the earth. I looked at it for a long time and this is what it told me. "As soon as I found the element which is indispensable for my life – love – in the air, why should I go on burying myself in the earth as my companions do? I have discovered a secret; I can draw all that I need for life from the air." So I meditated on this plant and I understood that people, too, are built to extract this love from the atmosphere and from the sun. In order to do this however, they must learn to develop their higher centres or chakras.

Love is an energy, a fluid, a quintessence, which exists throughout the universe: in oceans, rivers, mountains, rocks, grass and flowers, trees, earth and, above all, in the sun. Love is a cosmic energy of an unbelievable abundance and variety. God who is so generous, would never have decided that people could only find love in certain specific parts of their bodies. How very mean that would have been of Him! God is much more generous and liberal than that and so He put love everywhere. The ignorant who go on looking for love in men and women do not always find it, whereas Initiates who look for it in space are never deprived. For thousands of years people have looked at things in a different way and so they do not think it is possible to live and love without plunging their roots into the soil.

The search for love is fine, but why do you always look for it in the same old spots? If they are as amazing as they are thought to be, why don't you find love in abundance? There is a tiny bit of love there, but these few little particles are not enough to feed and quench the thirst of those who want to drink the whole ocean, and so, hungry and thirsty, you go off to look for it elsewhere.

Why do you always have to have a man or a woman in order to feel love? That is where limitations and unhappiness, difficulties and dependance come from. The veritable Masters cannot live without love, but they seek it, gather and draw it from all around them, and then they distribute it on all sides. They are plunged in love all the time : they breathe love, eat love, contemplate love, they think about love all the time. They have no need to look for a woman; they already have love, it is there, filling them up, it's marvellous, they are completely immersed in love! Why should they go and look for it elsewhere? Why should they wish to give up these feelings of abundance in exchange for burning coals on their heads?

I am not opposed to love, on the contrary, but I merely say that we must learn to find it everywhere, because love is everywhere, like the dew. Dew is vapourized water which is everywhere in the atmosphere and it only becomes visible when it condenses itself in the morning on plants. What is dew if not a kind of condensed love? What is a ray of the sun if not a kind of projected love? There you have it: everything in nature is love!

The true source of love is God Himself. A marvellous image of this heavenly source however is nearer us in the sun, which itself is immensely generous. All creation benefits by his presence, because with his love he constantly infuses life into herbs, plants, trees and vegetables, and we, in turn, receive life from them. The disciple who longs to know true life and love goes to the source, to the sun. By looking at the sun, and by meditating, by loving it, and letting it penetrate him more and more, he is like a fruit ripening in the sun, collecting particles of vitality. True love is not just embracing men and women and going to bed with them, but giving these particles to others so that they too can be vivified and enlightened.

The sun does not mean much to you yet, but when you are tired of weeping so many tears, and losing so many of your fine feathers, you will begin to look for the sun's love. At least with his love you will not suffer, for the sun takes nothing from you, but, on the contrary, gives to you. Men and women still need to suffer and so they do not look for love in the sun, but go on looking for their suffering amongst men and women. It's true! There at least they will be sure of finding it, together with all sorts of complications and botherations.... Whereas they will never find it near the sun... unless they go without a hat and then watch out for sunstroke!

Don't misunderstand me, I do not condemn sexual relations. My task is much more difficult than you can possibly imagine. I am an instructor, a spiritual guide and I put things in this way for those who are capable of going further in their understanding of love. As for the others, my God, let them do the best they can.

When I see someone who is built like a stallion, I do not tell him to live an ascetic life. I am not a fanatic, I realize that the question of love and sexuality has to be resolved by each person according to his nature. I must help those who want to perfect themselves by giving them methods, otherwise they may get led astray and that would be a pity. I have seen so many people who looked for something without knowing themselves quite what it was they were looking for and, as no one was able to enlighten them, they ended up lost.

Those who are married have obligations towards each other. I have always said that on this question of sexual relations, the couples must take their decisions, not independently, but together; unfortunately it does not often happen like this. Either the wife is unhappy because her husband suddenly decides to live like a hermit and regards her as an incarnation of the Devil or the husband suffers because the wife wants to be like an untouchable saint. It is desirable that men and women, even when married, should spiritualize and sublimate their love, but it must be with the agreement of both. Because there is so much misunderstanding, it is difficult to know how to deal with it. So I repeat that it is essential that both the husband and wife are in agreement; they must then proceed little by little, not giving up everything all at once, because if they do this they will become ill. If someone who has smoked four packets of cigarettes a day gives up smoking altogether he will suffer so much it will be sheer hell. But if he takes it progressively, his organism will adapt and one day he will be able to stop smoking without suffering. Yes indeed, you need to know how to proceed with everything.

Obviously I am not so naive as to think that what I am saying will apply to everybody. The sad reality is that there are barely two or three people amongst millions who are prepared to understand what love truly is and how to live it. Yet that is no reason for me not to enlighten those two or three, give them confidence and strength, so that instead of being in doubts and hesitation, and so going back to join the crowd of those who are weak, primitive and sensual, they can take heart. I have to talk, not for the whole world, but for those who are looking for new paths.

8

SPIRITUAL LOVE IS A HIGHER WAY OF FEEDING OURSELVES

Why do men and women seek each other out? It is because they are driven by hunger and they want to eat. In fact, love is a food, a drink; you can compare love to bread, to water, to wine.... Loving is exactly like eating: the same laws and processes operate. I have always said that if you have not understood the process of nutrition, neither will you understand the processes of love. As long as your reasons for eating are for mere nourishment, or because you are hungry or you like eating, and you make no effort to capture the etheric particles of the food, you will not be able to capture the etheric particles of the men and women you meet and your exchanges will be on a coarse level. You will behave like a caterpillar rather than a butterfly.

The Living Book of Nature teaches us much in the metamorphosis of caterpillar to butterfly. Nobody wants to look at a caterpillar very much because it is ugly, bloated, and moves about ponderously. Like all creatures, of course, it needs to eat, and it has a passion for leaves. It does not like fruit and flowers, but it loves those leaves which are absolutely indispensable for the tree's life. The light of the sun is transformed by the leaves and, by eating them, the caterpillar harms the tree, so that it is unable to produce flowers and fruit. So men do all they can to destroy caterpillars in their fields and gardens. What a life the caterpillar leads!

One fine day, we don't know why, the caterpillar begins to see that its life is not all that marvellous. It sees such beautifully coloured butterflies flitting through the sky that it feels ugly and disgusting by comparison; it realizes that because it is harmful, men are always trying to destroy it, so it decides to change and become something better. It decides to meditate, and because it needs peace and quiet, it begins by making a cocoon. It secretes a liquid which hardens into a tough thread... and that becomes silk! If silk is regarded as precious, it is undoubtedly because it was made in a meditative and spiritual state! (Silk garments are a very good protection against harmful fluids as are linen ones.)

So the caterpillar enters into a deep meditation... so deep that it sleeps. Lo and behold, in its subconscious – because even caterpillars have a subconscious – all the energies begin to work on that image of the butterfly which so impressed the caterpillar. (Real transformations are never achieved by thought in the conscious mind, but by the forces of the subconscious. If you want to achieve a desire you must know how to go down into your subconscious to leave the picture of what you want to achieve, otherwise who knows how long it will take to achieve it? The subconscious forces have the greatest power over matter.)

Time passes and, then, out of the cocoon where the caterpillar was encased, comes a butterfly. We must study this event in order to understand what Cosmic Intelligence teaches us by this change from caterpillar to butterfly. Up to a certain age, which can last for hundreds of incarnations, man is like the caterpillar who needs to eat leaves: he satisfies his own desires at the expense of others, he dirties them and tears them apart. But one day, disgusted with himself, he decides to change and become something better. He begins to concentrate, to meditate and, above all, to prepare a cocoon to protect himself... and this cocoon is his aura. The disciple who is aware of the power of the aura and works on it, will turn into a butterfly, or an Initiate, one day. He will stop eating other people – just as the caterpillar stopped eating leaves – and begin to feed himself on nectar and pollen, in other words, on

the finer emanations of people. You see the difference between an ordinary man and an Initiate
is in the different way they feed themselves.

Obviously for many 'caterpillars' this metamorphosis is not yet possible. They will tell you
that things should stay as they have done for the
past billion years. They do not realize that they
can become butterflies, winged beings that feed
on the most pure elements. Of course, you must
always go on eating, but there is food and food,
and different ways of eating. Instead of having
coarse, unaesthetic, even disgusting exchanges
with people, you can have delicate exchanges of
great love, as the butterfly does, without destroy-
ing or dirtying anything, without descending to
eating leaves.

So many young boys and girls come to tell
me that after certain experiences they have had,
they do not feel the same as before, they feel
weighed down and ill at ease. I tell them, "Do
not be annoyed at what I am going to say, but
your inner state is just like that of someone who
has gone through several chimney stacks; you
have stained and dirtied your etheric, astral and
mental garments." Yes, these experiences leave
imprints on your subconscious, invisible, of
course, but real, and when you want to make an
effort on the spiritual plane, you feel hindered,
fettered, weighed down, and held back. Before

they felt light, elated, happy and even proud, but now they are a little shrivelled and shamefaced. They do not have the same light on their face that they had before, and they all say, "I did not know it was like that. If only I had known!"

Oh yes, boys and girls throughout the world do not know, and do not want to know, what awaits them when they fling themselves into certain experiences. What they want is to have pleasure, to taste sensations, to be what they think is happy, but instead of happiness, shame, regret and a feeling of heavy darkness awaits them. The ignorance youth lives in is one of the greatest tragedies of humanity. When these youngsters come here to the Fraternity, they understand that there are truths to learn, laws to be obeyed, and they decide to give up the old way of life. How can they wipe out the traces of the life they led? Each day, they must wash themselves, purify themselves, work with the light, pray, meditate and link themselves to Heaven. Some time later, alas, not very quickly, they will begin to see a bit more clearly and progress.

May young people everywhere accept the guidance, enlightenment and instruction of the Initiates so that they stop rushing to throw themselves into useless and dangerous experiments. Then, my God, Heaven will send all the boys and all the girls exactly what suits each one of them. In any case, let no one accuse me of leading them astray. Look at the state all these boys and girls find themselves in when they have given way to premature experiences. They want to be happy and joyful, but they are only pretending. You feel that they do not have the same inspiration, something has broken in them, the light has been quenched. They ought to have realized that when you provoke volcanic eruptions in yourself, there are always consequences. Somewhere in their psychic structure, there have been explosions, ruptures and immense wastage of inestimably valuable quintessences.

You may say, "Well then, are we to have no pleasure, are we not to enjoy ourselves at all?" Yes, but you must know when, and in what way. Everything can become marvellous and magnificent when you know how to act and how to understand things. I have often compared the energy of the sexual force to petrol; it is the ignorant and the clumsy who are burnt by this force which uses up their quintessence, whereas the Initiates who know how to use it, fly through space. No other image sums up this question of the sexual force so well: the idiots are burnt and the intelligent fly through space! Why not fly through space, up to the stars, and know everything, instead of always being burnt?

I have never denied that there are good things in physical love. It is not up to me to criticize the workings of the Cosmic Intelligence. Not at all. But this Intelligence also foresaw an evolution of man and all other kingdoms. Certain manifestations of violence and cruelty which were seen as perfectly normal some centuries ago now outrage people who think such behaviour unworthy of man. So why should there not be an equal evolution in the way we look at love?

Those who know how to read find this evolution inscribed in the pages of the Living Book of Nature, in the story of the caterpillar and the butterfly, and also in the life of bees. Much has been written about bees, about the organization of their society and their customs, but not much has been said about them from the symbolic point of view. After bees have gathered nectar and pollen from flowers, they make that delicious food, honey. Symbolically, this work is that of Initiates or highly advanced disciples who take the most pure and subtle elements from the people they are with to make a honey which feeds the angels. Just as the bee does not eat the flowers, so the Initiate (unlike the majority of people) does not 'eat' people but only takes their most spiritual elements. With his alchemical knowledge, he is able to prepare in his heart and soul a quintessence, a food, a delicious perfume for the angels. So Initiates are symbolized by bees. In each human soul, even in those of criminals, the Initiate finds divine elements, and with all these elements he makes spiritual honey. A being who knows how to transform everything, sublimate everything, and illuminate everything is a bee. His hive is within and he makes honey from the purest and finest elements which he releases, his emanations.

Everyone has this task of extracting this quintessence and transforming it within themselves. They must learn how to do it by using their intellects, hearts and willpower; with these three elements they can achieve everything in their inner distilling flasks. Herein lies true alchemy. The only thing that the great Initiates, those true alchemists, teach is how to become a bee, how to extract the best from nature and above all from each person whom they look at, talk to and regard as a flower. Isn't it marvellous! Initiates discovered this philosophy inscribed throughout nature.

Joy, real joy, is not to be found in physical relationships. Take for example, two young lovers. At the beginning of their relationship they don't even kiss each other, but their lives are filled with such joy and inspiration! They get up in the morning and go to bed at night with only one thought in mind, that the other one exists, that they will meet and talk to each other. They write poetry, they exchange rose petals as though they were good luck charms.... But once they start to kiss and to sleep together, all the subtle side vanishes, they are no longer as happy, they do not think as much about one another and the troubles begin, the time has come for settling the accounts. At the beginning they were in Paradise. Why couldn't they have prolonged that state of bliss?

I know what you are going to say to me: you cannot go on nourishing yourself forever on homeopathic doses of smiles and words, you need something a bit more substantial. Fine, but do not be surprised at the results and do not go blaming anybody: you have made your bed, and now you must lie in it. Since you do not really want to live in poetry and in the light, since you want to have something more substantial, I do not say no, but I say beware.

My job is to explain, not to compel. My Teaching is like a table spread with all the fruits, vegetables, fishes and cheeses that exist... everything on earth is here, but that does not mean that everyone has to eat everything. I have to present all these truths to you, to give all the methods. It is up to you to choose what suits your stomach.

9

A HIGH IDEAL
TRANSFORMS SEXUAL ENERGY

People often come to ask me whether it is better to live in chastity or to have sexual relations. In fact this is not how the question should be asked; it is quite impossible to generalize about what is good or bad as it all depends on the individual. Living in chastity and continence can have very bad and also very good results. Continence can make some people hysterical, neurotic and ill, whereas it makes others strong, balanced and in good health. For some, it can do a lot of good to give a free rein to their sexual instinct, whereas it does others much harm. You must not judge things by saying, "This is good... but that is bad," as nothing of itself is either good or bad, but it changes according to how the forces are used and directed.

The important thing is to know first of all what your ideal is and what you want to become. If you want to learn how to sublimate your sexual energy so that you can make mighty discoveries in the spiritual world, you will obviously have to cut down some pleasures (or even give them up completely). If you do not have this high ideal, it is completely idiotic to control yourself, to be chaste and virginal and you will even become ill because all your efforts make no sense at all. It is clearly not reasonable to give the same advice and the same rules to everybody on this subject.

Someone may come to see me saying, "Master, I do not think that I should get married and have children as I am drawn to the spiritual life." When I look at him and see his constitution and structure, I reply, "No, no, it is much better for you to get married. If you don't, the results will be appalling! You will be unhappy and everybody will be upset by you." Somebody else may come who wants to get married and sometimes I say, "Get married if you want to, but you must know that as you are not built for marriage, you will suffer." So many boys and girls do not know themselves or what they are here for; each person has come to earth with a mission to fulfil, and it is not up to them to decide what their tendencies and instincts should be.

For example, try to explain to a cat that it should become a vegetarian and stop eating mice. It will listen to you and say, "Miaou," meaning, "Right, I understand, and I promise to give them up." But even whilst you are preaching to the cat it hears the tiny scratching noise of a mouse nibbling away at something.... Immediately, without a moment's remorse, the cat slinks off to pounce on the mouse. Yet it was listening so attentively to you, it even made you a promise! It comes back, licking its whiskers, and once again it says, "Miaou," meaning, "I couldn't help it, it's stronger than me (yes, this is a literal translation!), I can't change my catty nature from one day to the next." So you see, as long as one is a cat, one will go on eating mice.

This does not mean that you must not make any efforts to sublimate the sexual energy, but I have already explained to you that you must not try to fight against it as it will crush you. This is how you should deal with it; you must have a very powerful associate to whom you send this energy, and he, with his alchemical knowledge, will be able to change it into health, beauty, light and divine love. This associate is your high ideal; it is a fundamental idea which you live with, which you cherish and feed, and it, not you, will transform the energy. Those who have no spiritual ideal will never achieve this transformation and to them I can only say, "Find someone quickly and marry them, otherwise you will be a public nuisance!"

You see, I do not launch you on unknown seas; I put everything very clearly to you. If you do not want to become a magnificent being, a conductor of light, a benefactor of humanity, you will never manage to stifle this energy, so give it an outlet, get married and have children. If you do have this high ideal, it would be criminal to abandon Heaven to attempt to satisfy a husband or wife. It is worth the effort to work on a high ideal so that these energies can go to feed and strengthen it. When you feel a sexual impulse, concentrate on your ideal, and then this energy will go up to feed your brain; a few minutes later you will be free, you will have won!

I have spoken to you so often of the importance of having a high ideal. Today we have found another unexpected application in the sexual field. Make all your energies converge not towards pleasure but to a sublime ideal; then they will be able to serve you and contribute to the realization of that ideal. Though I have spoken to you about it, you have not yet understood what a powerful transformer of energies the high ideal is. So you must learn how to achieve it, how to give birth to it and how to feed it.

In fact, it is very simple. If you wish to improve, to be wiser, more radiant, purer and stronger, you must dedicate time to visualizing these longed for qualities. Imagine that you are

surrounded with light, that you are giving out
light to the whole world. Gradually, the pictures
you form of these qualities will become living,
they will work on you, they will transform you,
because they will be drawing all the necessary
elements from the universe so that you can become steeped in them. Of course, a lot of time
and work is necessary before you get results, but
when they come, you will be in no doubt: you
will feel a living entity with you who protects
and teaches you, who purifies and enlightens
you and, when you are in difficult situations,
brings you all the elements you need. First of all
you must visualize and create this perfection on
the mental plane and then it will descend to ma-
terialize on the physical plane.

Let me make myself clear! I am not so nar-
row-minded and fanatical as you may think. I
am liberal, very liberal. However, given my task
as teacher, I have to show you what is best, and
despite your protests that it is not possible to do
as I say, I assure you that you will succeed in a
future incarnation. Don't go committing suicide
with the excuse that you could not obtain the results you wanted! I have to show you new possi-
bilities, new paths, and it's up to you to choose
how you tackle them; but if you cannot manage
them at the moment, I am not going to throttle
you! My job is to give explanations; each one

must choose according to his nature, his temperament, and his level of evolution.

I have been given this work to do with you because Heaven knows that I am liberal, and that I will not lead you astray. It is not my fault if someone is incapable of working in this direction; because he has not worked in his past incarnations he now meets enormous difficulties. I must give the methods for those who are already prepared so that they can go further, for if I do not give them, who else will?

Love is precious, love is essential, but in order to strengthen it, to protect it, and to make it durable, you must diminish its physical manifestations. However, you must also know that it is very dangerous for the nervous system to give up one joy without finding a replacement for it. You must always replace a pleasure with another, more spiritual, pleasure, if you are to save yourself from negative reactions.

In Initiatic Science it is said that renouncement should not be a deprivation, but rather a replacement, a transposition into another world. The same activity continues, but with purer, more luminous, materials. When I say that one should deprive one's self, give things up and make sacrifices, it is only a manner of speaking. In fact, one should never deprive oneself, one should simply take oneself away to a higher region to continue doing whatever one did: instead of drinking swamp water full of germs, drink crystalline water from a pure spring. If you stop drinking, you'll die. A true Master never deprives himself of anything: he eats, drinks, breathes, and loves, but in realms and in states of consciousness unknown to the ordinary man.

The way most people generally try to get rid of their habit of smoking, drinking, their need for women, is by suppressing the desire without putting something else in its place, and this is extremely dangerous for they are thrown off balance and plunged into a void. There must be a compensation, you must substitute a higher desire for your lower desire. So think very carefully each time you decide to give up a need that is very strong in you, for it is a very serious decision to make. The need should be replaced, and to satisfy it, you should go on eating, drinking, loving and living, but on a level that no longer exposes you to the same dangers. If you do not find a substitute for your desires, you will fall once again.

Initiates are built like everyone else and if they did not find joy and greater pleasure in their meditations, contemplations, the way they live, and in their love for people, they would never be able to be victorious. Their great love for a high ideal enables them to sublimate their energies.

Never battle against sexual instincts with willpower alone. In order to conquer, you need to call on heavenly forces, on a high ideal, on a mighty love for perfection, purity and beauty. Without this high ideal, for a divine and perfect life, you will be broken in your struggle against the sexual force. Repression is no answer, because repression is just the refusal to give the sexual force its normal outlet without an ideal which works on the higher planes to sublimate this force.

You can put your trust in me, I know what I am talking about. I say nothing to you which I have not first verified myself, and it is because I have verified all these great laws that I have the right to speak to you. For more than forty years I have been giving you guidelines which, if understood properly, will never cause any havoc. All my life I have been doing experiments on myself in order to observe and discover the best methods, and so I can now be extremely useful to you. If you have no faith in me, if you are afraid that applying these methods will make you unhappy, then ignore them; I have nothing against that, but you will be the one to suffer. One day you will see how stupid you have been to have acted so carelessly without even recognizing what your true interests were.

10

OPEN YOUR LOVE TO A HIGHER PATH

Initiates teach us that at the beginning of the world, only the Absolute existed. Kabbalistic tradition calls the Absolute, Ain Soph Aur, or Light Unlimited. One can only say about this unknowable, inconceivable entity that it is both Being and Non-Being – only silence can express it. It contains all powers and when it wished to manifest Itself, It emanated a part of Itself. But for this manifestation to become possible, It had to polarize Itself into positive and negative, masculine and feminine, for without polarization there can be no manifestation. So the two principles appeared by polarization and with these two principles God created everything. It would obviously take too long to explain this question in detail, but in a few words I can say that the subtle, luminous and systematically arranged world emanated by the Absolute is the world of 'creation,' Heaven and the Spirit; in its turn, this world of creation was condensed and concretized in successive stages in order to give the world of 'formation,' of matter, the physical plane.

In order to express this truth, one of the greatest Initiates, Hermes Trismegistus, gave us the phrase, "That which is below is like that which is above." He wanted to show that if one knew how to reason correctly and really understood that which is below on the physical plane, one could also know that which is above on the plane of Ideas, of forces and powers, of all that is invisible and subtle. Since, on the physical plane, men and women are a reflection of these masculine and feminine principles which exist above, we have to conclude that God, who is the masculine principle, must also possess the feminine pole and so He too, must have a wife, though Christianity teaches us that God only has a Son.

In all religions the Cosmic Spirit, God, has a Wife; in the Kabbalah she is called Shekinah. God's Wife is Nature; together they have children. In all religions you find this trinity: in India it is Brahma, Prakriti and Purusha; in Egyptian religion it is Osiris, Isis and Horus. Christianity is an exception because of a widespread, erroneous opinion that only the masculine is perfect. In the past, fathers were often furious when a daughter was born, and for many Christians, women are creatures of the Devil because Eve seduced Adam. Once again this misunderstanding of the Bible should be corrected. God has a Wife, as without the feminine principle there would be no creation; nothing can live and blossom in nature without both these principles participating. Since we are created in the image and likeness of God, we must once again reinstate the feminine principle in all its equal perfection and splendour to its true place.

However, let us go back to the three persons of the Holy Trinity represented in the Christian religion by the Father, the Son, and the Holy Ghost. The first principle represents power, the source of all life; the second principle represents light and understanding, and the third principle, the Holy Spirit, is the principle of love. Yes, the Holy Spirit is the fire of love.

It says in the Scriptures that all sins will be forgiven except the sin against the Holy Ghost, and this is because the sin against the Holy Ghost is the sin against love. Christianity has never known how to explain what this sin is and why it cannot be forgiven, but today, fully aware of my responsibility, I want to throw light on this question.

Everyone accepts that if you lack understanding or willpower, you will keep coming up

against checks and disillusionments in life, yet
you do not think it is serious, that any harm will
be done, or difficulties arise, if you do not have
the right concepts or behaviour in love. Ah yes, I
see. To be stupid is serious, to be weak is serious, yet to make love like an animal is not serious? What absurd reasoning! It is precisely this
fault which is not forgiven, because it has such
deplorable consequences; one cannot be forgiv-
en for it, but one is punished and one has to pay.
"Pay? How?" As soon as you feel certain sensations, as soon as you allow certain pleasures,
you are burning materials and therefore you are
starting to pay.

All physiological manifestations are a com-
bustion. Merely by thinking and talking you
burn materials and, even more so, when you
have a great joy or sorrow, your emotions burn
up materials that leave behind their ashes. It
takes much time to recuperate the expense of
energy used in each manifestation, emotion and
feeling. How can you possibly imagine that in all
the ferment of love, you expend nothing and lose
nothing? It is precisely where the expenditure is
the greatest that it is the most difficult to
retrieve; all the most useful quintessences essential for life and health have been consumed in
the furnace.

I am not suggesting that you should suppress

everything and live a life without love, not at all, but you should live a sensible, intelligent, and aesthetic life. There is reason to be astonished and even shocked when you see how people wallow in physical pleasure without trying to add another, more spiritual, element; they are losing so much in all areas. They are unaware that they are losing anything and they excuse themselves by saying, "These organs never wear out." Of course, they do not wear out, but you should realize that there is a material in the brain which is used up very quickly by thoughtless sensuality.

I hope no Christians will be shocked by what I am now going to say to you. According to the science of symbols, the Heavenly Father is linked to the brain; Christ is linked to the solar plexus (which is the real heart); the Holy Spirit is linked to the genital organs. For the first time, I reveal this mystery to you: the Holy Spirit is linked to love and to the genital organs. So in order not to commit errors and then to be punished, we must learn to have the right attitude to these organs which God has given us. I myself think that there is nothing more marvellous, more intelligent and more profound than the organs of men and women. You, too, must esteem them, appreciate them, and even consecrate them to God.

In Initiatic Science, we learn that the sexual force comes from Heaven, even if it manifests itself in a very imperfect way through the genitals. I do not agree with those who say, "Love is no more than two skins rubbing together." They are only looking at the results, but the cause, the origin, of this energy comes from very far away and so escapes them. In fact, without this energy, no amount of rubbing together would do anything. Yes, love is a divine force which comes from on high and must therefore be treated with respect; we should think how to conserve it and think how we can send it back up to Heaven instead of sending it to Hell where it feeds monsters, phantoms and elementals. We must learn to send this force back up again, but people are too preoccupied to stop and study this science. They feel this terrible tension and they say they are compelled to get rid of the pressure as quickly as possible. Why don't they understand that this tension is the greatest of riches?

Think of the human being as a building with fifty, a hundred, or even a thousand floors; you need a very high pressure to get the water up to the people living on the top floor. Men and women must know and use this tension to feed and water the cells of their brains, for the Cosmic Intelligence has constructed a special network to channel this energy right up to the brain. Just because science has not yet discovered this network does not mean one has the right to deny its existence.

When men and women waste this sacred energy without respect, without real love, and without the desire to realize sublime creations, they are committing the sin against the Holy Spirit, and this sin is very widespread these days. Where are the men and women who will once more regard love as a force which restores, recreates, shows the way and truly enables them to become divinities? Man will return to Paradise through love but, unfortunately, it is by love that man is going farther and farther away from Paradise today.

Once and for all, let this be quite clear to you. According to the way you behave towards love and the genital organs, you will enter – or fail to enter – into harmony with the Sublime Being which is the cosmic Holy Spirit, you will once again find the Kingdom of God within you, or you will transgress its laws. You can therefore draw this conclusion: the same organs are capable of taking you down to Hell or lifting you to Heaven, it all depends on how you direct your energies.

It is written in the Emerald Tablet, "From earth it rises, from Heaven it falls, it receives power both from the higher forces and from the lower forces.... It is the most forceful of all forces." The normal course of this force is from Heaven to earth and from earth back to Heaven.

Do not suppress, confine, or repress love, but find methods and means to manifest it correctly. Love is an energy which comes from very high; it is of the same essence as the sun and man's job is to capture this energy and make it circulate within him, sending it back up to Heaven.

When God created men and women, he equipped them with the most amazing network of channels through which the sexual force, if you know how to direct it, can find its path upwards. Everyone has these installations, but they have so neglected them that they are rusty, blocked and disconnected. Moreover, as these channels have a fluidic nature, they are much finer than those of the nervous system; only clairvoyants can see them and discern the course which these energies follow as they surge from very low down and are guided upwards to feed the brain.

Understand what I am saying; Initiates make no attempt to hinder this energy as it courses downwards. Only idiotic puritans fight against this energy, and they are always hurled to the ground and crushed by it, because they are fighting against a divine principle, against the solar force, against the river of life which is the Christ itself (Christ said, "I am the way, the truth and the life.") When there are layers of impurity on man, accumulated there by all his uncontrollable passions, this energy cannot rise toward Heaven, it buries itself in the ground and all is lost. When a man is pure, when he is master of himself, when he is truly linked to God, this energy, which never stops pouring down each day, will not get lost, but will take its path upwards once again. An uninterrupted circulation flows from above to below and up again.

Once man understands all God's works, and sees how the world is made, that we begin and end with Heaven, the world will no longer be an obstacle for him. Love comes from Heaven and is bound to return there. There are not two or three or four loves, it is always one and the same, even though it may be understood and lived at different levels. People say that God is love, but they never say the Devil is love.... Love comes from God and if, when it descends, it encounters no resistance, it will circulate freely without any fevers or burnings. A love that burns is a love whose path is blocked. (You need only compare this with being in bed with a fever: this fever is caused by impurities which hindered the circulation of your blood and your life force. As your organism struggles to eliminate all these obstacles, fever is produced.)

Sexual energy comes from above and the whole aim is to send it back up again. This will be possible when you no longer are preoccupied with hunting for pleasure, but devote yourself to work. I repeat that the real tragedy of mankind is that they have not understood that this energy of love is not merely destined for pleasure, but that it is there to awaken certain faculties which will permit them to do a psychic and spiritual work of the greatest importance, a work which will allow them to become conductors of this mighty force which will transform the world, which changes cinders and lead into gold, which makes precious stones and diamonds. This transformation can only be made by the power of love, not by any other means. From now on, search for the attitude, the thoughts, feelings and plans which you should have so that this divine energy can be controlled and guided.

The time has come when the mysteries of love should be understood in light, in peace, joy, wonder, and with perfect balance, not in huge volcanic eruptions. Get ready to do a divine work for the whole of humanity: that is what Heaven is expecting of you, that you should work. What do you do with your love? You only use it for pleasure and that is why its energies turn to poison. From now on, think of sending love back up to its source, say, "Lord God, I consecrate these energies to Your glory and for the coming of Your Kingdom... here they are!"

Where are the men and women who will dedicate their love to Heaven? People think that the exchanges they make only concern themselves. If they eat, it is for themselves and Heaven has nothing to do with it. This "I," this "me" that they want to satiate with sensuality is already a part of Hell. They suppress all thoughts of Heaven with the excuse that what they are doing is shameful (so why are they doing it?) and that Heaven shouldn't see them. They hide nothing in front of Hell, they have no shame and so Hell comes to their banquet. Even the Church has not given any explanations but contents itself with repeating, "Increase and multiply," and so everybody couples in the shadows, to Hell's delight. People speak of the sacrament of marriage, but, in fact, even when men and women marry according to the rules, they give themselves over to excesses in their marital relations and all Hell is invited to partake. There they are in bed trying out all sorts of positions to get the greatest possible number of sensations, gorging themselves like animals, and this is supposed to be the 'sanctity of marriage.' Poor misguided humanity!

I understand that the physical side of mar-

riage is important and that it can even help you
to find the spiritual side, but you must learn to
regard it as a starting point, not as a goal. Let us
imagine that you feel a physical attraction towards a man or a woman: fine, but instead of
diving into that feeling so that you drown in it,
use the attraction as an opportunity to advance,
to make spiritual progress. Suppose you see a
show, read a book, or flip through a magazine
which releases certain reactions in you; instead
of letting yourself get carried away and then
foundering, take that situation as a starting
point, a spring-board, and try to propel yourself
high in divine contemplation. When you come
back down again you will be staggered to see
what treasures you have just collected and also
amazed that what originally disturbed you in
fact ended up as a stimulant, help, and encour-
agement, to your progress.

Whenever you feel a disturbing sensation,
don't just give yourself up to it blindly without
knowing where you are going. Remember that in
Initiatic Science everything is used: so rejoice
and thank Heaven saying, "Lucky me! I have
been given an amazing blessing! This is the kind
of situation which makes everyone else tear their
hair and yield to temptation, but where I have a
chance of triumphing. Thank you, Lord! I understand. Let's both tackle it together!" and

then you use the methods I have given you. In this way, you get into the habit of triumphing over everything, nothing disturbs or conquers you, and you become strong, powerful, you become a divinity. But no, people let themselves drift along blindly with the excuse that they are 'impelled.' Of course, everyone is 'impelled'... but there are different directions in which you can be impelled, and it is much better to be impelled towards the heights.

Where do you think human love comes from if it is not from God Himself? We say, "God is Love," but which love? People differentiate between physical, sensual love and divine love. In fact there is no difference: it is the same force, the same energy which comes from very high up, but it is a question of degree. You do not really understand what the number 1 is, indivisible, inseparable, 1. Love is precisely that: the number 1, and it is 1 which produces all the other numbers: 2, 3, 4 are only manifestations of 1, other degrees or forms of 1. God is 1, love is 1, God is love. Everything which is not 1 is in reality just another aspect of 1. We must return to unity, we should go back to the centre, to God, to the love that is 1, instead of staying out on the periphery in multiplicity.

When I say to you that we must send love back towards Heaven, it is because love must return to its source. People have not understood what the phrase "God is love" means, just as they have not understood the word 'unity' or what it means to return to this unity. It is crystal clear for me. Unity is God, God is love, and we must return to this love.

By the same author:

Izvor Collection

201 - Toward a Solar Civilization
It is not enough to be familiar with the astronomical theory of heliocentricity. Since the sun is the centre of our universe, we must learn to put it at the centre of all our preoccupations and activities.

202 - Man, Master of His Destiny
If human beings are to be masters of their own destiny, they must understand that the laws which govern their physical, psychic and spiritual life are akin to those which govern the universe.

203 - Education Begins Before Birth
Humanity will improve and be transformed only when people realize the true import of the act of conception. In this respect, men and women have a tremendous responsibility for which they need years of preparation.

204 - The Yoga of Nutrition
The way we eat is as important as what we eat. Through our thoughts and feelings, it is possible to extract from our food spiritual elements which can contribute to the full flowering of our being.

205 - Sexual Force or the Winged Dragon
How to master, domesticate and give direction to our sexual energy so as to soar to the highest spheres of the spirit.

206 - A Philosophy of Universality
We must learn to replace our restricted, self-centred point of view with one that is immensely broad and universal. If we do this we shall all benefit; not only materially but particularly on the level of consciousness.

207 - What is a Spiritual Master
A true spiritual Master is, first, one who is conscious of the essential truths written by cosmic intelligence into the great book of Nature. Secondly, he must have achieved complete mastery of the elements of his own being. Finally, all the knowledge and authority he has acquired must serve only to manifest the qualities and virtues of selfless love.

208 - Under the Dove, the Reign of Peace
Peace will finally reign in the world only when human beings work to establish peace within themselves, in their every thought, feeling and action.

209 - Christmas and Easter in the Initiatic Tradition
Human beings are an integral part of the cosmos and intimately
concerned by the process of gestation and birth going on in nature.
Christmas and Easter – rebirth and resurrection – are simply two ways
of envisaging humanity's regeneration and entry into the spiritual life.

210 - The Tree of the Knowledge of Good and Evil
Methods, not explanations, are the only valid answers to the problem
of evil. Evil is an inner and outer reality which confronts us every day,
and we must learn to deal with it.

211 - Freedom, the Spirit Triumphant
A human being is a spirit, a spark sprung from within the Almighty.
Once a person understands, sees and feels this truth, he will be free.

212 - Light is a Living Spirit
Light, the living matter of the universe, is protection, nourishment
and an agency for knowledge for human beings. Above all, it is the
only truly effective means of self-transformation.

213 - Man's Two Natures, Human and Divine
Man is that ambiguous creature that evolution has placed on the
borderline between the animal world and the divine world. His nature
is ambivalent, and it is this ambivalence that he must understand and
overcome.

214 - Hope for the World: Spiritual Galvanoplasty
On every level of the universe, the masculine and feminine principles
reproduce the activity of those two great cosmic principles known
as the Heavenly Father and the Divine Mother of which every
manifestation of nature and life are a reflection. Spiritual galvano-
plasty is a way of applying the science of these two fundamental
principles to one's inner life.

215 - The True Meaning of Christ's Teaching
Jesus incorporated into the Our Father – or Lord's Prayer – an ancient
body of knowledge handed down by Tradition and which had existed
long before his time. A vast universe is revealed to one who knows
how to interpret each of the requests formulated in this prayer.

216 - The Living Book of Nature
Everything in nature is alive and it is up to us to learn how to
establish a conscious relationship with creation so as to receive that
life within ourselves.

217 - New Light on the Gospels
The Parables and other tales from the Gospels are here interpreted as
situations and events applicable to our own inner life.

218 - The Symbolic Language of Geometrical Figures

Each geometrical figure – circle, triangle, pentagram, pyramid or cross – is seen as a structure fundamental to the organization of the macrocosm (the universe) and the microcosm (human beings).

219 - Man's Subtle Bodies and Centres

However highly developed our sense organs, their scope will never reach beyond the physical plane. To experience richer and subtler sensations, human beings must exercise the subtler organs and spiritual centres that they also possess: the aura, the solar plexus, the Hara centre, the Chakras, and so on.

220 - The Zodiac, Key to Man and to the Universe

Those who are conscious of being part of the universe feel the need to work inwardly in order to find within themselves the fullness of the cosmic order so perfectly symbolized by the Zodiac.

221 - True Alchemy or The Quest for Perfection

Instead of fighting our weaknesses and vices – we would inevitably be defeated – we must learn to make them work for us. We think it normal to harness the untamed forces of nature, so why be surprised when a Master, an initiate, speaks of harnessing the primitive forces within us? This is true spiritual alchemy.

222 - Man's Psychic Life: Elements and Structures

"Know thyself" How to interpret this precept carved over the entrance to the temple at Delphi? To know oneself is to be conscious of one's different bodies, from the denser to the most subtle, of the principles which animate these bodies, of the needs they induce in one, and of the state of consciousness which corresponds to each.

223 - Creation: Artistic and Spiritual

Everyone needs to create but true creation involves spiritual elements. Artists, like those who seek the spirit, have to reach beyond themselves in order to receive elements from the higher planes.

224 - The Powers of Thought

Thought is a power, an instrument given to us by God so that we may become creators like himself – creators in beauty and perfection. This means that we must be extremely watchful, constantly verifying that what we do with our thoughts is truly for our own good and that of the whole world. This is the one thing that matters.

225 -Harmony and Health
Illness is a result of some physical or psychic disorder. The best defence against illness, therefore, is harmony. Day and night we must take care to be attuned and in harmony with life as a whole, with the boundless life of the cosmos.

226 - The Book of Divine Magic
True, divine magic, consists in never using the faculties, knowledge, or powers one has acquired for one's own self-interest, but always and only for the establishment of God's kingdom on earth.

227 - Golden Rules for Everyday Life
Why spoil one's life by chasing after things that matter less than life itself? Those who learn to give priority to life, who protect and preserve it in all integrity, will find more and more that they obtain their desires. For it is this, an enlightened, luminous life that can give them everything.

228 - Looking into the Invisible
Meditation, dreams, visions, astral projection all give us access to the invisible world, but the quality of the revelations received depends on our efforts to elevate and refine our perceptions.

229 - The Path of Silence
In every spiritual teaching, practices such as meditation and prayer have only one purpose: to lessen the importance attributed to one's lower nature and give one's divine nature more and more scope for expression. Only in this way can a human being experience true silence.

230 - The Book of Revelations: A Commentary
If *Revelations* is a difficult book to interpret it is because we try to identify the people, places and events it describes instead of concentrating on the essence of its message: a description of the elements and processes of our spiritual life in relation to the life of the cosmos.

231 - The Seeds of Happiness
Happiness is like a talent which has to be cultivated. Those who want to possess happiness must go in search of the elements which will enable them to nourish it inwardly; elements which belong to the divine world.

232 - The Mysteries of Fire and Water
Our psychic life is fashioned every day by the forces we allow to enter us, the influences that impregnate us. What could be more poetic, more meaningful than water and fire and the different forms under which they appear?

233 - Youth: Creators of the Future

Youth is full of life, enthusiasms and aspirations of every kind. The great question is how to channel its extraordinary, overflowing effervescence of energies.

234 - Truth, Fruit of Wisdom and Love

We all abide by our own "truth", and it is in the name of their personal "truth" that human beings are continually in conflict. Only those who possess true love and true wisdom discover the same truth and speak the same language.

235 - In Spirit and in Truth

Since we live on earth we are obliged to give material form to our religious beliefs. Sacred places and objects, rites, prayers and ceremonies are expressions of those beliefs. It is important to understand that they are no more than expressions – expressions which are always more or less inadequate. They are not themselves the religion, for religion exists in spirit and in truth.

236 - Angels and Other Mysteries of the Tree of Life

God is like a pure current of electricity which can reach us only through a series of transformers. These transformers are the countless luminous beings which inhabit the heavens and which tradition calls the Angelic Hierarchies. It is through them that we receive divine life; through them that we are in contact with God.

237 - Cosmic Balance, the Secret of Polarity

Libra – the Scales – symbolizes cosmic balance, the equilibrium of the two opposite and complementary forces, the masculine and feminine principles, by means of which the universe came into being and continues to exist. The symbolism of Libra, expression of this twofold polarity, dominates the whole of creation.

By the same author
(translated from the French)

"Complete Works" Collection

Brochures:
New Presentation

Live Recordings on Tape

KC2510An — The Laws of Reincarnation
(Two audio cassettes)

(available in French only)

K 2001 Fr — La science de l'unité
K 2002 Fr — Le bonheur
K 2003 Fr — La vraie beauté
K 2004 Fr — L'éternel printemps
K 2005 Fr — La loi de l'enregistrement
K 2006 Fr — La science de l'éducation
K 2007 Fr — La prière
K 2008 Fr — L'esprit et la matière
K 2009 Fr — Le monde des archétypes
K 2010 Fr — L'importance de l'ambiance
K 2011 Fr — Le yoga de la nutrition
K 2012 Fr — L'aura
K 2013 Fr — Déterminisme et indéterminisme
K 2014 Fr — Les deux natures de l'être humain
K 2015 Fr — Prendre et donner
K 2016 Fr — La véritable vie spirituelle
K 2017 Fr — La mission de l'art
K 2018 Fr — Il faut laisser l'amour véritable se manifester
K 2019 Fr — Comment orienter la force sexuelle
K 2020 Fr — Un haut idéal pour la jeunesse
K 2021 Fr — La réincarnation – Preuves de la réincarnation
dans les Évangiles.
K 2022 Fr — La réincarnation – Rien ne se produit par hasard,
une intelligence préside à tout.
K 2023 Fr — La réincarnation – L'aura et la réincarnation.
K 2024 Fr — La loi de la responsabilité
K 2551 Fr — La réincarnation (coffret de 3 cassettes)
K 2552 Fr — Introduction à l'astrologie initiatique
(coffret de 3 cassettes)
K 2553 Fr — La méditation (coffret de 3 cassettes)

World Wide - Editor-Distributor
Editions PROSVETA S.A. - B.P. 12 - F - 83601 Fréjus Cedex (France)
Tel. (00 33) 04 94 40 82 41 - Fax (00 33) 04 94 40 80 05
Web: **www.prosveta.com**
E-mail: **international@prosveta.com**

Distributors

AUSTRALIA
SURYOMA LTD
P.O. Box 798 – Brookvale – N.S.W. 2100
Tel. / Fax: (61) 2 9984 8500 – E-mail: suryoma@csi.com
AUSTRIA
HARMONIEQUELL VERSAND – A-5302 Henndorf, Hof 37
Tel. / Fax: (43) 6214 7413 – E-mail: info@prosveta.at
BELGIUM
PROSVETA BENELUX – Liersesteenweg 154 B-2547 Lint
Tel.: (32) 3/455 41 75 – Fax: 3/454 24 25
N.V. MAKLU Somersstraat 13-15 – B-2000 Antwerpen
Tel.: (32) 3/321 29 00 – E-mail: prosveta@skynet.be
VANDER S.A. – Av. des Volontaires 321 – B-1150 Bruxelles
Tel.: (32) 27 62 98 04 – Fax: 27 62 06 62
BRAZIL
NOBEL SA – Rua da Balsa, 559 – CEP 02910 - São Paulo, SP
BULGARIA
SVETOGLED – Bd Saborny 16 A, appt 11 – 9000 Varna
E-mail: svetgled@revolta.com
CANADA
PROSVETA Inc. – 3950, Albert Mines – North Hatley, QC J0B 2C0
Tel.: (1) 819 564-8212 – Fax: (1) 819 564-1823
In Canada, call toll free: 1-800-854-8212
E-mail: prosveta@prosveta-canada.com — www.prosveta-canada.com
COLUMBIA
PROSVETA – Avenida 46 no 19-14 (Palermo) – Santafé de Bogotá
Tel.: (57) 232-01-36 – Fax: (57) 633-58-03
CYPRUS
THE SOLAR CIVILISATION BOOKSHOP
73 D Kallipoleos Avenue - Lycavitos – P.O. Box 4947, 1355 – Nicosia
Tel.: 02 377503 and 09 680854
CZECH REPUBLIC
PROSVETA Tchèque – Ant. Sovy 18 – České Budejovice 370 05
Tel. / Fax: 0042038-53 00 227 – E-mail: prosveta@seznam.cz
GERMANY
PROSVETA Deutschland – Postfach 16 52 – 78616 Rottweil
Tel.: (49) 741 46551 – Fax: (49) 741 46552 – E-mail: Prosveta.de@t-online.de
EDIS GmbH, Mühlweg 2 – 82054 Sauerlach
Tel.: (49) 8104-6677-0 – Fax: (49) 8104-6677-99
GREAT BRITAIN & IRELAND
PROSVETA – The Doves Nest, Duddleswell Uckfield – East Sussex TN 22 3JJ
Tel.: (44) (01825) 712988 – Fax: (44) (01825) 713386
E-mail: prosveta@pavilion.co.uk

GREECE
PROSVETA – VAMVACAS INDUSTRIAL EQUIPEMENT
Moutsopoulou 103 – 18541 Piraeus
HAITI
B.P. 115 – Jacmel, Haiti (W.I .) – Tel. / Fax: (509) 288-3319
HOLLAND
STICHTING PROSVETA NEDERLAND
Zeestraat 50 – 2042 LC Zandvoort – E-mail: prosveta@worldonline.nl
HONG KONG
SWINDON BOOK CO LTD
246 Deck 2, Ocean Terminal – Harbour City – Tsimshatsui, Kowloon
ISRAEL
ÉDITIONS GALATAIA – 58 Bar-Kohva street – Tel Aviv
Tel.: 00 972 3 5286264 – Fax: 00 972 3 5286260
ITALY
PROSVETA Coop. – Casella Postale – 06060 Moiano (PG)
Tel. / Fax: (39) 075-8358498 – E-mail: prosveta@tin.it
LUXEMBOURG
PROSVETA BENELUX – Liersesteenweg 154 - B-2547 Lint
NORWAY
PROSVETA NORDEN – Postboks 5101 – 1503 Moss
Tel.: 69 26 51 40 – Fax: 69 25 06 76
E-mail: prosveta Norden – prosnor@online.no
PORTUGAL
PUBLICAÇÕES EUROPA-AMERICA Ltd
Est Lisboa-Sintra KM 14 – 2726 Mem Martins Codex
ROMANIA
ANTAR – Str. N. Constantinescu 10 – Bloc 16A - sc A - Apt. 9
Sector 1 – 71253 Bucarest
Tel.: (40) 1 679 52 48 – Tel. / Fax: (40) 1 231 37 19
RUSSIA
Neapolitensky – 40 Gorohovaya - Appt 1 – Saint-Petersbourg
Tel.: (70) 812 5327 184 / (70) 812 2726 876 – Fax: (70) 812 1582 363
SINGAPORE & MALAYSIA
AMERICASIA GLOBAL MARKETING – Clementi Central Post Office
P.O. Box 108 – Singapore 911204 – Tel.: (65) 892 0503 – Fax: (65) 95 199 198
E-mail: harvard1@mbox4.singnet.com.sg
SPAIN
ASOCIACIÓN PROSVETA ESPAÑOLA – C/ Ausias March n° 23 Ático
SP-08010 Barcelona — Tel.: (34) (3) 412 31 85 – Fax: (34) (3) 302 13 72
SWITZERLAND
PROSVETA Société Coopérative – CH - 1808 Les Monts-de-Corsier
Tel.: (41) 21 921 92 18 – Fax: (41) 21 922 92 04
E-mail: prosveta@swissonline.ch
UNITED STATES
PROSVETA U.S.A. – P.O. Box 1176 – New Smyrna Beach, FL.32170-1176
Tel. / Fax: (904) 428-1465
E-mail: sales@prosveta-usa .com — www.prosveta-usa.com
VENEZUELA
BETTY MUÑÕZ – Urbanización Los Corales – avenida Principal
Quinta La Guarapa – LA GUAÏRA – Municipio Vargas

Printed by
Imprimerie H.L.N.
Sherbrooke (Quebec) Canada
in March 2000